ULYSSES S. GRANT

ULYSSES S. GRANT

Steven O'Brien

CHELSEA HOUSE PUBLISHERS
NEW YORK
PHILADELPHIA

Chelsea House Publishers

EDITOR-IN-CHIEF: Remmel Nunn
MANAGING EDITOR: Karyn Gullen Browne
COPY CHIEF: Juliann Barbato
PICTURE EDITOR: Adrian G. Allen
ART DIRECTOR: Maria Epes
DEPUTY COPY CHIEF: Mark Rifkin
ASSISTANT ART DIRECTOR: Loraine Machlin
MANUFACTURING MANAGER: Gerald Levine
SYSTEMS MANAGER: Lindsey Ottman
PRODUCTION MANAGER: Joseph Romano
PRODUCTION COORDINATOR: Marie Claire Cebrián

World Leaders—Past & Present
SENIOR EDITOR: John W. Selfridge

Staff for ULYSSES S. GRANT
ASSOCIATE EDITOR: Terrance Dolan
COPY EDITOR: Brian Sookram
EDITORIAL ASSISTANT: Martin Mooney
PICTURE RESEARCHER: Lisa Kirchner
DESIGNER: David Murray
ASSISTANT DESIGNER: Diana Blume
COVER ILLUSTRATION: Robert Caputo

3 5 7 9 8 6 4 2

Library of Congress Cataloging-in-Publication Data

O'Brien, Steven.
    Ulysses S. Grant/Steven O'Brien.
    p.   cm.—(World leaders—past and present)
    Includes bibliographical references and index.
    Summary: Follows the life of the war hero who became the
eighteenth president of the United States.
    ISBN 1-55546-809-8
          0-7910-0696-4 (pbk.)
    1. Grant, Ulysses S. (Ulysses Simpson), 1822–85—Juvenile
literature. 2. Presidents—United States—Biography—Juvenile
literature. 3. Generals—United States—Biography—Juvenile
literature. 4. United States. Army—Biography—Juvenile literature. [1.
Grant, Ulysses S. (Ulysses Simpson), 1822–85. 2. Presidents.] I. Title.
II. Series: World leaders past & present.
E672.027   1991
973.8′2′092—dc20   90–35963
[B]   CIP
[92]   AC

Contents

John Adams
John Quincy Adams
Konrad Adenauer
Alexander the Great
Salvador Allende
Marc Antony
Corazon Aquino
Yasir Arafat
King Arthur
Hafez al-Assad
Kemal Atatürk
Attila
Clement Attlee
Augustus Caesar
Menachem Begin
David Ben-Gurion
Otto von Bismarck
Léon Blum
Simon Bolívar
Cesare Borgia
Willy Brandt
Leonid Brezhnev
Julius Caesar
John Calvin
Jimmy Carter
Fidel Castro
Catherine the Great
Charlemagne
Chiang Kai-Shek
Winston Churchill
Georges Clemenceau
Cleopatra
Constantine the Great
Hernán Cortés
Oliver Cromwell
Georges-Jacques
  Danton
Jefferson Davis
Moshe Dayan
Charles de Gaulle
Eamon De Valera
Eugene Debs
Deng Xiaoping
Benjamin Disraeli
Alexander Dubček
François & Jean-Claude
  Duvalier
Dwight Eisenhower
Eleanor of Aquitaine
Elizabeth I
Faisal
Ferdinand & Isabella
Francisco Franco
Benjamin Franklin

Frederick the Great
Indira Gandhi
Mohandas Gandhi
Giuseppe Garibaldi
Amin & Bashir Gemayel
Genghis Khan
William Gladstone
Mikhail Gorbachev
Ulysses S. Grant
Ernesto "Che" Guevara
Tenzin Gyatso
Alexander Hamilton
Dag Hammarskjöld
Henry VIII
Henry of Navarre
Paul von Hindenburg
Hirohito
Adolf Hitler
Ho Chi Minh
King Hussein
Ivan the Terrible
Andrew Jackson
James I
Wojciech Jaruzelski
Thomas Jefferson
Joan of Arc
Pope John XXIII
Pope John Paul II
Lyndon Johnson
Benito Juárez
John Kennedy
Robert Kennedy
Jomo Kenyatta
Ayatollah Khomeini
Nikita Khrushchev
Kim Il Sung
Martin Luther King, Jr.
Henry Kissinger
Kublai Khan
Lafayette
Robert E. Lee
Vladimir Lenin
Abraham Lincoln
David Lloyd George
Louis XIV
Martin Luther
Judas Maccabeus
James Madison
Nelson & Winnie
  Mandela
Mao Zedong
Ferdinand Marcos
George Marshall

Mary, Queen of Scots
Tomáš Masaryk
Golda Meir
Klemens von Metternich
James Monroe
Hosni Mubarak
Robert Mugabe
Benito Mussolini
Napoléon Bonaparte
Gamal Abdel Nasser
Jawaharlal Nehru
Nero
Nicholas II
Richard Nixon
Kwame Nkrumah
Daniel Ortega
Mohammed Reza Pahlavi
Thomas Paine
Charles Stewart
  Parnell
Pericles
Juan Perón
Peter the Great
Pol Pot
Muammar el-Qaddafi
Ronald Reagan
Cardinal Richelieu
Maximilien Robespierre
Eleanor Roosevelt
Franklin Roosevelt
Theodore Roosevelt
Anwar Sadat
Haile Selassie
Prince Sihanouk
Jan Smuts
Joseph Stalin
Sukarno
Sun Yat-sen
Tamerlane
Mother Teresa
Margaret Thatcher
Josip Broz Tito
Toussaint L'Ouverture
Leon Trotsky
Pierre Trudeau
Harry Truman
Queen Victoria
Lech Walesa
George Washington
Chaim Weizmann
Woodrow Wilson
Xerxes
Emiliano Zapata
Zhou Enlai

CHELSEA HOUSE PUBLISHERS

ON LEADERSHIP

Arthur M. Schlesinger, jr.

LEADERSHIP, it may be said, is really what makes the world go round. Love no doubt smooths the passage; but love is a private transaction between consenting adults. Leadership is a public transaction with history. The idea of leadership affirms the capacity of individuals to move, inspire, and mobilize masses of people so that they act together in pursuit of an end. Sometimes leadership serves good purposes, sometimes bad; but whether the end is benign or evil, great leaders are those men and women who leave their personal stamp on history.

Now, the very concept of leadership implies the proposition that individuals can make a difference. This proposition has never been universally accepted. From classical times to the present day, eminent thinkers have regarded individuals as no more than the agents and pawns of larger forces, whether the gods and goddesses of the ancient world or, in the modern era, race, class, nation, the dialectic, the will of the people, the spirit of the times, history itself. Against such forces, the individual dwindles into insignificance.

So contends the thesis of historical determinism. Tolstoy's great novel *War and Peace* offers a famous statement of the case. Why, Tolstoy asked, did millions of men in the Napoleonic Wars, denying their human feelings and their common sense, move back and forth across Europe slaughtering their fellows? "The war," Tolstoy answered, "was bound to happen simply because it was bound to happen." All prior history predetermined it. As for leaders, they, Tolstoy said, "are but the labels that serve to give a name to an end and, like labels, they have the least possible connection with the event." The greater the leader, "the more conspicuous the inevitability and the predestination of every act he commits." The leader, said Tolstoy, is "the slave of history."

Determinism takes many forms. Marxism is the determinism of class. Nazism the determinism of race. But the idea of men and women as the slaves of history runs athwart the deepest human instincts. Rigid determinism abolishes the idea of human freedom—

the assumption of free choice that underlies every move we make, every word we speak, every thought we think. It abolishes the idea of human responsibility, since it is manifestly unfair to reward or punish people for actions that are by definition beyond their control. No one can live consistently by any deterministic creed. The Marxist states prove this themselves by their extreme susceptibility to the cult of leadership.

More than that, history refutes the idea that individuals make no difference. In December 1931 a British politician crossing Park Avenue in New York City between 76th and 77th Streets around 10:30 P.M. looked in the wrong direction and was knocked down by an automobile—a moment, he later recalled, of a man aghast, a world aglare: "I do not understand why I was not broken like an eggshell or squashed like a gooseberry." Fourteen months later an American politician, sitting in an open car in Miami, Florida, was fired on by an assassin; the man beside him was hit. Those who believe that individuals make no difference to history might well ponder whether the next two decades would have been the same had Mario Constasino's car killed Winston Churchill in 1931 and Giuseppe Zangara's bullet killed Franklin Roosevelt in 1933. Suppose, in addition, that Adolf Hitler had been killed in the street fighting during the Munich *Putsch* of 1923 and that Lenin had died of typhus during World War I. What would the 20th century be like now?

For better or for worse, individuals do make a difference. "The notion that a people can run itself and its affairs anonymously," wrote the philosopher William James, "is now well known to be the silliest of absurdities. Mankind does nothing save through initiatives on the part of inventors, great or small, and imitation by the rest of us—these are the sole factors in human progress. Individuals of genius show the way, and set the patterns, which common people then adopt and follow."

Leadership, James suggests, means leadership in thought as well as in action. In the long run, leaders in thought may well make the greater difference to the world. But, as Woodrow Wilson once said, "Those only are leaders of men, in the general eye, who lead in action. . . . It is at their hands that new thought gets its translation into the crude language of deeds." Leaders in thought often invent in solitude and obscurity, leaving to later generations the tasks of imitation. Leaders in action—the leaders portrayed in this series—have to be effective in their own time.

And they cannot be effective by themselves. They must act in response to the rhythms of their age. Their genius must be adapted, in a phrase of William James's, "to the receptivities of the moment." Leaders are useless without followers. "There goes the mob," said the French politician hearing a clamor in the streets. "I am their leader. I must follow them." Great leaders turn the inchoate emotions of the mob to purposes of their own. They seize on the opportunities of their time, the hopes, fears, frustrations, crises, potentialities. They succeed when events have prepared the way for them, when the community is awaiting to be aroused, when they can provide the clarifying and organizing ideas. Leadership ignites the circuit between the individual and the mass and thereby alters history.

It may alter history for better or for worse. Leaders have been responsible for the most extravagant follies and most monstrous crimes that have beset suffering humanity. They have also been vital in such gains as humanity has made in individual freedom, religious and racial tolerance, social justice, and respect for human rights.

There is no sure way to tell in advance who is going to lead for good and who for evil. But a glance at the gallery of men and women in *World Leaders—Past and Present* suggests some useful tests.

One test is this: Do leaders lead by force or by persuasion? By command or by consent? Through most of history leadership was exercised by the divine right of authority. The duty of followers was to defer and to obey. "Theirs not to reason why / Theirs but to do and die." On occasion, as with the so-called enlightened despots of the 18th century in Europe, absolutist leadership was animated by humane purposes. More often, absolutism nourished the passion for domination, land, gold, and conquest and resulted in tyranny.

The great revolution of modern times has been the revolution of equality. The idea that all people should be equal in their legal condition has undermined the old structure of authority, hierarchy, and deference. The revolution of equality has had two contrary effects on the nature of leadership. For equality, as Alexis de Tocqueville pointed out in his great study *Democracy in America*, might mean equality in servitude as well as equality in freedom.

"I know of only two methods of establishing equality in the political world," Tocqueville wrote. "Rights must be given to every citizen, or none at all to anyone . . . save one, who is the master of all." There was no middle ground "between the sovereignty of all and the absolute power of one man." In his astonishing prediction of 20th-century totalitarian dictatorship, Tocqueville explained how the revolution of equality could lead to the *"Führerprinzip"* and more terrible absolutism than the world had ever known.

But when rights are given to every citizen and the sovereignty of all is established, the problem of leadership takes a new form, becomes more exacting than ever before. It is easy to issue commands and enforce them by the rope and the stake, the concentration camp and the *gulag*. It is much harder to use argument and achievement to overcome opposition and win consent. The Founding Fathers of the United States understood the difficulty. They believed that history had given them the opportunity to decide, as Alexander Hamilton wrote in the first Federalist Paper, whether men are indeed capable of basing government on "reflection and choice, or whether they are forever destined to depend . . . on accident and force."

Government by reflection and choice called for a new style of leadership and a new quality of followership. It required leaders to be responsive to popular concerns, and it required followers to be active and informed participants in the process. Democracy does not eliminate emotion from politics; sometimes it fosters demagoguery; but it is confident that, as the greatest of democratic leaders put it, you cannot fool all of the people all of the time. It measures leadership by results and retires those who overreach or falter or fail.

It is true that in the long run despots are measured by results too. But they can postpone the day of judgment, sometimes indefinitely, and in the meantime they can do infinite harm. It is also true that democracy is no guarantee of virtue and intelligence in government, for the voice of the people is not necessarily the voice of God. But democracy, by assuring the right of opposition, offers built-in resistance to the evils inherent in absolutism. As the theologian Reinhold Niebuhr summed it up, "Man's capacity for justice makes democracy possible, but man's inclination to injustice makes democracy necessary."

A second test for leadership is the end for which power is sought. When leaders have as their goal the supremacy of a master race or the promotion of totalitarian revolution or the acquisition and exploitation of colonies or the protection of greed and privilege or the preservation of personal power, it is likely that their leadership will do little to advance the cause of humanity. When their goal is the abolition of slavery, the liberation of women, the enlargement of opportunity for the poor and powerless, the extension of equal rights to racial minorities, the defense of the freedoms of expression and opposition, it is likely that their leadership will increase the sum of human liberty and welfare.

Leaders have done great harm to the world. They have also conferred great benefits. You will find both sorts in this series. Even "good" leaders must be regarded with a certain wariness. Leaders are not demigods; they put on their trousers one leg after another just like ordinary mortals. No leader is infallible, and every leader needs to be reminded of this at regular intervals. Irreverence irritates leaders but is their salvation. Unquestioning submission corrupts leaders and demeans followers. Making a cult of a leader is always a mistake. Fortunately hero worship generates its own antidote. "Every hero," said Emerson, "becomes a bore at last."

The signal benefit the great leaders confer is to embolden the rest of us to live according to our own best selves, to be active, insistent, and resolute in affirming our own sense of things. For great leaders attest to the reality of human freedom against the supposed inevitabilities of history. And they attest to the wisdom and power that may lie within the most unlikely of us, which is why Abraham Lincoln remains the supreme example of great leadership. A great leader, said Emerson, exhibits new possibilities to all humanity. "We feed on genius. . . . Great men exist that there may be greater men."

Great leaders, in short, justify themselves by emancipating and empowering their followers. So humanity struggles to master its destiny, remembering with Alexis de Tocqueville: "It is true that around every man a fatal circle is traced beyond which he cannot pass; but within the wide verge of that circle he is powerful and free; as it is with man, so with communities."

1

A Thousand Deaths for General Lee

There is nothing left for me to do," said Confederate general Robert E. Lee, "but to go and see General Grant." It was the morning of April 9, 1865, and Lee's Army of Northern Virginia, once the most feared combat force on the continent, was surrounded on all sides by the Union forces of General Ulysses S. Grant. Lee knew that he was beaten. He briefly considered committing suicide — "I have only to ride along the line and all will be over" — but decided it was his honorable duty to represent the Confederacy in this dark hour. He dispatched a messenger with a brief note accepting Grant's terms and began to prepare for the final confrontation with his enemy. The general put on a magnificent new uniform with an embroidered belt, shining, high black boots with red silk stitching, gold spurs, a crimson sash, and a gilded sword. Then, although he would "rather face a thousand deaths," Lee mounted his white horse and set out for the small Virginia town of Appomattox Courthouse, where he would surrender his proud army to General Grant.

The pain in my head seemed to leave the moment I got Lee's letter.
—ULYSSES S. GRANT

Lieutenant General Ulysses S. Grant, commander of all the Union armies. In March 1864, President Lincoln put the entire federal war effort in the hands of Grant. By the spring of 1865, Grant had a stranglehold on the armies of the Confederacy.

General Robert E. Lee, commander of the Confederate Army of Northern Virginia. In April 1865, Lee's army found itself hopelessly surrounded by the forces of Grant.

Lee's messenger turned the letter over to a Union lieutenant, who went in search of General Grant. Almost two hours later, the lieutenant found Grant on a country road a few miles away from Union headquarters. Grant, who had spent a mostly sleepless night battling one of the migraine headaches that frequently tormented him, was standing beside his horse and smoking a cigar, seemingly lost in thought. He read Lee's note. The lieutenant, well aware of the momentous nature of the missive, watched his general's face closely, but Grant remained impassive. He finished reading the letter, sat down in the grass, quickly wrote a reply, and handed it to the lieutenant. He watched the messenger gallop away and then mounted his own horse. His headache was fading. He lit a fresh cigar and set out at a trot for Appomattox.

Lee was already at the designated farmhouse when Grant arrived; this was Grant's moment, and he had kept his defeated counterpart waiting for more than an hour — the privilege of the victor. The two generals could not have presented a more symbolically disparate appearance. The dignified, white-bearded Lee, his decorations flashing in the morning sunlight, was the embodiment of the Southern aristocracy. In his spotless, elaborate new uniform, his shining sword conspicuous at his side, he waited for Grant with an almost regal bearing. There was nothing aristocratic about Grant. He was the republican in plain Union blue, unshaven, his boots dusty, a cigar in his mouth, his uniform rumpled as if it had been slept in the night before (it had been) and devoid of medals, ribbons, or any other military accoutrements. Grant wore a cavalryman's weathered hat, carried no sword, and dismounted with the casual ease of the expert horseman. He was a short, slight man who slouched a bit, and as he walked toward General Lee there seemed to be nothing remarkable about him at all, except for his eyes, which were of a wintry gray and which seemed to contain both a childlike innocence and a terrible knowledge.

On the morning of April 9, 1865, Union lieutenant Charles E. Pease, carrying a message from General Lee accepting Grant's terms of surrender, went in search of General Grant. Pease found Grant on a country road, standing beside his horse Cincinnati and smoking a cigar.

This was the man who had crushed the glorious Confederate rebellion; this was the scourge of Tennessee, the cruel, relentless warrior of the Virginia Wilderness campaign, the man who had unleashed "total war" on Georgia and South Carolina; this was the greatest military hero in the history of the United States since George Washington. A failed businessman, a failed farmer, a soldier who had at one time been drummed out of the army, a drunkard, he was now being compared to Napoleon Bonaparte and Hannibal, and President Abraham Lincoln would laud him as "the defender of the Republic." Soon, his fellow citizens would elevate him to an even higher command — the presidency. General Lee watched the small man in the dusty blue uniform approach, studied him curiously for any outward sign of greatness, and steeled himself for the moment when he would surrender his splendid sword to him. Finally, after four years of terrible conflict, the two generals stood face to face. The assembled officers of the Confederacy and the Union watched in silence. Grant took the cigar from his mouth and smiled at Lee. The Civil War was over.

The McLean house outside the village of Appomattox Courthouse, Virginia, was chosen as the sight for the meeting between Grant and Lee that would end the war between the states.

His parents did not name him until six weeks after his birth on April 27, 1822, in Point Pleasant, Ohio. His mother, Hannah Simpson Grant, wanted to call him Albert, but her parents and husband disagreed. Finally, everyone scribbled his or her favorite suggestion on a piece of paper and placed it in a hat. It was a fittingly haphazard way to name a man who would lead an oddly haphazard life. As Grant himself put it shortly before his death, "Circumstances always did shape my course different from my plans." Ulysses, the Latin name for the ancient Greek hero Odysseus, who was endlessly buffeted about by the whims of the gods, was drawn. The matter seemed settled, but then grandfather Simpson became deeply depressed because his name, Hiram, had not been selected. The boy's father, Jesse Root Grant, settled the matter by naming the child Hiram Ulysses Grant.

General Robert E. Lee (right) shakes hands with General Grant in the parlor of the McLean house, surrendering the beaten Army of Northern Virginia to Grant and thus ending the Southern rebellion.

Point Pleasant, Ohio, where Ulysses Grant was born, on April 27, 1822. The Grant family moved to Georgetown, Ohio, shortly after the birth of Ulysses.

The Grants were an odd bunch, by all accounts. Jesse Root Grant was an ambitious, overly talkative fellow who ran a tannery for most of his life, dabbled in politics, and engaged in endless gossip with his neighbors. His wife, Hannah Simpson Grant, was an enigma. She was strangely silent and withdrawn and rarely came out of the house; those who knew her believed she was a bit "touched." Even when her first son became the most famous man in America as commander of the Union armies and then as president, she remained hidden and unphotographed, giving no interviews and sequestering herself in the small brick house in Ohio while the rest of the family resided in the White House or nearby. Grant himself seldom mentioned her.

Eighteen months after the birth of Ulysses, the young family — Jesse and Hannah would eventually have 5 children, 3 girls and 2 boys — moved 25 miles east to the newly developing county seat of Georgetown, Ohio. Jesse had saved enough money to build his own tannery and, across the street, a small, neat brick house. He quickly won a solid business success and opened a livery stable. It was there, in and around sleepy Georgetown, that Ulysses spent his boyhood. He was an amiable, if somewhat shy and quiet boy, and an adequate student. The focal point of both his and his father's life was horses. But Ulysses and his father could not have been farther apart in their relationship to these creatures.

For Jesse Grant, horses were grist for his business; they were slaughtered for their hides, which were converted to leather products in his tannery.

One of the few existing photographs of Grant's mother, Hannah Simpson Grant. Mrs. Grant was a mysterious woman who never left her house and refused to speak with reporters even after her son had become president.

But to Ulysses, horses were wonderful beings. And the animals seemed to sense in Ulysses his love for them; it was a well-known fact in Georgetown that Ulysses Grant had a way with horses. Clients from out of town were frequently alarmed to see the tiny boy toddling among the legs of the horses in Jesse's stables, pulling on their tails and laughing happily, but the beasts never so much as stepped on the little fellow's toes. As he grew older, Ulysses came to hate the tannery; to him, it was a place of death, of buckets of blood and screaming horses. Jesse Grant had his faults but he was never a tyrant to his children, and he let Ulysses handle all the chores that had to be done outside the tannery, among the living horses.

Horses, rather than boys and girls, were the companions of Ulysses Grant in his youth, and he found them to be simple creatures, loyal, predictable, and devoid of certain aspects of the human character with which Ulysses Grant never quite came to terms. If you treated a horse right, the horse always responded in kind. Once you made a friend of a horse, the horse would never betray you. People, on the other hand, were different. In all matters — except for the relatively straightforward matter of war, which reduced relations between men to their crudest and most direct form — Ulysses Grant suffered from a certain naïveté in his dealings with his fellow men and women.

A story from his youth aptly demonstrates this side of Grant's personality, which became most evident when he was engaged in interactions of a financial or commercial nature. Young Grant — he was about eight years old at the time — had his eye on a beautiful colt belonging to a Mr. Ralston, who lived just outside Georgetown. Jesse gave his son $25 and instructed him in the basics of bargaining: He was to offer Ralston $20 for the colt; if Ralston would not sell for that price, Ulysses was to offer $22.50; if Ralston still refused to sell, Ulysses could then offer him $25. Ulysses eagerly rode off to Ralston's house, where he promptly informed the man that "Papa says I may offer you $20 for the colt, but if you won't take that, I am to offer $22 and a half, and if you won't take that, I am to give you $25."

> *My family is American, and has been for generations, in all its branches, direct and collateral.*
> —ULYSSES S. GRANT

The merciless Ralston not only took the boy's $25, he informed Jesse of his son's blunder. Jesse, perhaps in an attempt to embarrass Ulysses into learning a lesson, perhaps simply because he could never keep his mouth shut, spread the story around, and soon Ulysses found himself the butt of his peers' jokes — bargaining for a horse was a ritual of manhood, and Ulysses had failed miserably, even comically. His classmates nicknamed him "Useless." Although Grant remembered this incident with considerable anguish to his dying day, he never seemed to learn a lesson from it, and his overly trusting nature and lack of business sense would be the bane of his adult life as well.

Ulysses Grant's father, Jesse Root Grant, was a tanner and a small-time politician. Unlike his silent wife and taciturn son, Jesse was a garrulous fellow whose loose tongue frequently caused trouble for Ulysses.

Ulysses Grant may not have been able to haggle for a horse very well, but everyone in Georgetown, even the truculent Jesse, had to admit that nobody could ride one like Ulysses. Restless in school and always yearning for the outdoors, he passed his youth and early teenage years in the company of horses, and he was never so happy as when he was riding a good horse alone across the Ohio country-side. He did not like to bother anyone and was content when no one bothered him. As he got older, he developed some vague ambitions about becoming a farmer or trader or perhaps going to college. Jesse felt that none of these was likely to occur, so he used his political and business connections to procure an appointment to the United States Military Academy at West Point for his eldest son. Ulysses received the news that he was to become a cadet with his usual equanimity. He had no strong feelings either way concerning the issue, and at least now he would have a chance to get out of Georgetown and see some of the country.

The U.S. Military Academy at West Point, New York. Grant's father obtained an appointment to the academy for his son in the winter of 1839, and the 17-year-old Grant arrived at West Point in the spring.

The 17-year-old, slender, 5-feet 1-inch Ulysses arrived at West Point in the spring of 1839. One of the first things he obtained at the academy was a new name of sorts. Because of a clerical error, he was listed under the name U. S. Grant, rather than H. U. Grant. Deciding he liked the sound of U. S. Grant, Ulysses did not bother to correct the mistake. Upperclassmen promptly nicknamed him "Uncle Sam." Soon, the Uncle Sam got shortened to Sam, and Ulysses had a new first name. Sam was the name those who knew him at West Point always called him. But the initials *U. S.* would come to stand for a nickname of a much more fateful significance.

"Sam" Grant's four years at West Point were entirely unremarkable. He quickly settled into the middle academic range of his class and remained there. He found military life stifling and dreary and hated the emphasis placed upon saluting, jumping to attention, shining boots, and marching. He had been born tone deaf and lacked any sense of rhythm, and no matter how hard he tried, he could not learn how to march in step, or to dance. Attending balls, an important part of a young cadet's social grooming, was something he avoided whenever possible. Grant was anything but a rebel, however, and his presence at West Point was a wholly inconspicuous one. Later, during the Civil War, many of his Union comrades and Confederate adversaries were men who had attended West Point at the same time Grant had, but most of them had absolutely no recollection of Grant at the academy. Those who did remember him, aside from his few personal friends, recalled him only for his gifts as a horseman.

Grant was grateful when his four years at West Point came to an end. He had decided long before graduation that he would become a college math teacher as soon as he had finished the obligatory tour of duty as a second lieutenant. He applied for the cavalry, but because there were no openings in the tiny American army for a cavalry officer at that time, he was assigned to the Fourth Infantry, stationed at Jefferson Barracks, St. Louis, Missouri.

Thus ended Grant's time at West Point. Seemingly, none of his peers or superiors was ever given to the thought that an exceptional, indeed, an unprecedented military future awaited young Grant. But Grant himself had already experienced his own quiet sense of foreshadowing: One day during Grant's first year at the academy, General Winfield Scott visited and conducted a review of the cadets. Grant was much taken with the general's appearance, and, as he wrote later, he experienced "a presentiment for a moment that some day I should occupy his place in review."

Given leave for 10 weeks after graduation, Grant returned home for a visit before heading on to St. Louis. Taller now — about five feet, seven inches — and with handsome features, he decided to show off his dress uniform. As Grant rode proudly down the main street of Georgetown, the town drunk

A painting of American Indians done by West Point cadet Ulysses Grant. Bored with military life — it "had no charms for me," Grant wrote — he passed some of the time by reading and painting.

mocked him by parading barefoot after him in a pair of ragged blue pants with a strip of white cotton sewn on the sides. "The joke was a huge one in the mind of many of the people," Grant wrote, "and was much enjoyed by them; but I did not appreciate it so highly." When he got home, he put his uniform away for the duration of his visit.

There was not much for young officers to do at Jefferson Barracks. The commanding officer believed in making life comfortable for his junior officers: If an officer did his daily tasks and was present for drill and roll call, the rest of his time he was on his own. Grant and a friend from West Point, Frederick Dent, began spending a good deal of their free time at Dent's nearby family home, White Haven. The Dents, descendants of a Maryland clan, fancied themselves members of the southern gentry and liked to think of the comfortable White Haven as a southern plantation-estate. At the Dent home, Grant experienced the full measure of "southern" hospitality. Mrs. Dent treated her son's army companion like a member of the family, and Grant quickly became a regular dinner guest. He loved riding with the Dent children. The youngest of them, seven-year-old Emma, developed a crush on him.

The oldest Dent girl, 17-year-old Julia, was away attending school in St. Louis. When she returned home, Grant was smitten. Julia was a short, plump young woman who loved to be outdoors, where she could indulge her passions for riding, fishing, hiking, and hunting. Although she pretended to be passive, as was expected of young women in her time, she actually had tremendous willpower and courage. But it was Julia's superb equestrian skills that first caught Grant's attention. She was someone he could ride with who could match his own skill. They were soon going off on long rides together on the pretext of visiting neighbors. Grant became her constant companion. "He was always by my side," Julia would later recall, "walking or riding." Grant soon noticed that he hated being away from Julia, and as he put it himself, he "understood the reason without explanation from anyone." The first campaign of Ulysses S. Grant was about to begin.

2

Without a Scratch

One of my superstitions had always been when I started to go anywhere, or do anything, not to turn back, or stop until the thing intended was accomplished." For Grant, this philosophy was applicable to matters of love as well as to matters of war. Consequently, although Julia Dent initially rebuffed his advances, the young West Point graduate courted her with determination and the appropriate degree of gallantry — once, he risked drowning by fording a rain-swollen river on horseback to be at her side — and she soon began to yield. But before "the thing intended" could be "accomplished," as Grant put it, he was called by a mistress of a much harsher nature — war. For the next four years, Grant would continue his courtship of Julia Dent, but he would do so by letter.

You can have but little idea of the influence you have over me, even while so far away. If I feel tempted to do anything that I think is not right I am sure to think, "Well now if Julia saw me would I do so" and thus it is absent or present I am more or less governed by what I think is your will.
—ULYSSES S. GRANT
in a letter to Julia Dent

In 1845, Second Lieutenant Ulysses S. Grant, along with the Fourth Infantry Regiment of the U.S. Army, sailed to Corpus Christi, Texas, part of the territory disputed by Mexico and the United States. The presence of U.S. troops in the area provoked a confrontation with Mexico, and Grant experienced combat for the first time.

Tensions along the Mexican-American border had been strained since the Republic of Texas had seceded from Mexico in 1836. President James K. Polk, a firm believer in the doctrine of Manifest Destiny (the belief that the United States was inevitably destined to expand to the Pacific Ocean), was elected president in 1845, and he wasted no time in annexing Texas and making it part of the United States. The Mexican government perceived this as a belligerent act — Mexico had never officially recognized the independence of Texas. But Polk's belligerence had only just begun; he had his eye on the Mexican territory that today encompasses the entire American Southwest. Polk made a halfhearted attempt to buy these lands from Mexico, and when the Mexicans turned down the offer, he decided to provoke a war and take the territory by force. An army of 3,000 men, under the command of General Zachary Taylor, was sent to do the job. Among these men was Lieutenant Ulysses S. Grant.

Grant had no illusions about Polk's little war, and his analysis of the situation was keen, incisive, and completely devoid of the nationalist sentiment and expansionist fervor that was prevalent in the United States at the time. According to Grant, the Mexican War "was one of the most unjust ever waged by a stronger against a weaker nation. It was an instance of a republic following the bad example of European monarchies, in not considering justice in their desire to acquire additional territory." Taylor's mission was to goad the Mexican army patrolling the Rio Grande into a fight so that President Polk could secure a "self-defense" declaration of war from Congress. As Grant put it, "We were sent to provoke a fight, but it was essential that Mexico should commence it." Although he harbored moral compunctions, Grant never considered resigning his commission or requesting a transfer. He possessed an innate sense of loyalty to the United States, and although it lacked any jingoistic enthusiasm, it was entirely unshakable.

Taylor's army set out on its 150-mile march from the Texas port of Corpus Christi to Matamoros, on the Rio Grande, in early March, 1846. For Grant,

the march was something of a vacation. The army proceeded at a leisurely pace and was entirely unmolested by Mexicans or Indians. The soldiers ate well, for there was an abundance of game, although Grant could not bring himself to shoot any of it like the other men. Grant loved the rolling prairies, the sunshine, and the clear, crisp air of Texas, and he was awed and delighted at the sight of a herd of wild horses so large that he estimated it could easily fill the entire state of Delaware. As the march progressed, the lieutenant gained weight, took on a healthy, ruddy complexion, and got rid of a nagging, tubercular cough that had bothered him for years.

The Mexican troops avoided the American soldiers for as long as possible, but finally, one day along the Rio Grande, they fired on an American patrol. Having been provided with the necessary "provocation," Congress declared war, and General Taylor swung his small army into action. For Lieutenant Grant, the events that followed were, up to that point, the most pivotal of his life, and they played a large part in forming the characteristics that would eventually help him win the Civil War.

General Zachary Taylor (on horseback), known as Old Rough and Ready to his troops, at the Battle of Buena Vista, February 22, 1847. Grant admired Taylor's informal style of leadership and eventually adopted it as his own.

Grant saw action for the first time at the Battle of Palo Alto, May 8, 1846. "There is no great sport in having bullets flying about one in every direction," Grant wrote of the experience, "but I find they have less horror when among them than when in anticipation."

On the afternoon of May 8, 1846, the American force encountered a Mexican force of about 6,000 men. The two armies confronted one another at Palo Alto, Texas. The Mexican lines bristled with bayonets and lances, which, as Grant later recalled, "glistened in the sunlight formidably." Although his troops were outnumbered two to one, General Taylor knew that he had the superior artillery and muskets, and he initiated an attack. Using the tall grass for cover, the Americans advanced on the Mexicans, who opened fire with muskets and cannons. This was Grant's first combat experience. His matter-of-fact description of the battle provides the first hint of the almost preternatural sense of calm that was to serve him so well in later, infinitely more bloody engagements: "There was a brisk fire upon our troops, and some execution was done. One cannonball passed through our ranks, not far from me. It took off the head of an enlisted man, and the under jaw of Captain Page of my regiment, while the splinters from the musket of the killed soldier, and his brains and bones, knocked down two or three others, including one officer, Lieutenant Wallen — hurting them more or less."

In this his first battle, Grant also displayed a quality that all great generals have shown throughout the history of war — initiative. As cannonballs crashed through the tall grass and musket balls buzzed angrily overhead, Grant took command of a company of infantrymen and led a charge. The Mexicans retreated before the assault, and Grant and his men took several prisoners, including a colonel. Although his actions were extraordinary for a man facing pitched battle for the first time, Grant downplayed them in his memoirs: "The ground had been charged over before. My exploit was equal to that of the soldier who boasted that he had cut off the leg of one of the enemy. When asked why he did not cut off his head, he replied, 'Some one had done that before.' This left no doubt in my mind but that the battle would have been won, just as it was, if I had not been there." Grant certainly had not cut off anybody's head, but he had displayed something for which he would become famous and even infamous —a willingness to fight.

The Mexican army retreated to the city of Monterrey, with Taylor's troops in hot pursuit. Grant, assigned quartermaster's duty, was responsible for supervising many of the mules and horses that carried the supplies the army needed. A quartermaster's job virtually guaranteed that he would have to stay with the wagons that followed behind the army. But Grant had gotten a taste of combat at Palo Alto, found that he liked it, and was eager for more. When the American artillery began firing on Monterrey, he disregarded orders and rode forward to see what was happening. The men he joined were ordered to attack, and Grant went with them.

Grant survived this initial assault on Monterrey, although a third of his companions did not. Having penetrated the city, he found himself in the midst of bloody house-to-house fighting. As the Americans pushed toward the center of town, they were caught in a murderous cross fire; the Mexicans fired from roofs, windows, church steeples, and door- and alleyways. Soon, the men Grant was with were pinned down and low on ammunition. Grant volunteered to ride back out through the city to secure help for the wounded and more ammunition. He put one foot in a stirrup, clung to the side of the saddle, and, using the horse's body as a shield, rode at breakneck speed through the hail of Mexican fire. "I got out safely," he wrote later, "without a scratch." Monterrey surrendered the following day.

General Taylor's victories at Palo Alto and Monterrey had generated a great deal of publicity back in the States, and the newspapers were calling him a hero. President Polk, afraid—and rightly so—that Taylor's rising fame might make him a political rival, decided to allow Winfield Scott to command another army in Mexico. (Scott was the general whose appearance at West Point in 1839 had triggered Grant's presentiment of greatness.) Scott was a huge, flamboyant, and occasionally brilliant general who had first made a name for himself in the War of 1812. Grant's regiment was reassigned to Scott's army, and in the early spring of 1847 Scott commenced his Mexican campaign.

Convinced that Taylor's strategy of attacking Mexico's northern cities would only prolong the war, Scott decided to make a direct assault on the capital, Mexico City. His plan for a quick, decisive victory entailed transporting his army by ship down the Gulf of Mexico to Veracruz, the major supply port for Mexico City, and then marching inland along the same route that the Spanish conquistador Hernán Cortés had followed several hundred years before in his conquest of the Aztec Empire. General Scott liked the idea that he would be following Cortés's route; like the Spaniard, Scott hoped to take Mexico City with a force that would be vastly outnumbered and cut off from any support.

Scott's campaign was brilliantly planned and executed. His force landed unopposed in Mexico. Veracruz was quickly occupied, and in April the army began its long march toward the capital. The Mexicans offered periodic resistance, and battles were fought at Cerro Gordo, Contreras, Churubusco, and Molino del Rey. The Americans prevailed in all of these contests, but the one that impressed Grant the most was the Battle of Cerro Gordo, where Scott faced potential disaster in a heavily defended, treacherous mountain pass. Through a series of daring nighttime maneuvers, in which men, supplies, horses, and artillery were hauled by rope up and down the steep cliffs of Cerro Gordo, Scott succeeded in outflanking the Mexicans and taking them by surprise. "Perhaps there was not a battle of the Mexican war, or of any other, where orders issued before an engagement were nearer being a correct report of what afterwards took place," Grant wrote in admiration. "The surprise of the enemy was complete, the victory overwhelming."

The American army reached the outskirts of Mexico City in late August. Chapultepec, the heavily fortified citadel guarding the approach to the city, was assaulted on September 8. Again, Grant pitched himself into the center of the fray. Chapultepec capitulated, but only after a bitter struggle.

American artillery brigades shell the Mexican port of Veracruz in March 1847. The city capitulated after a six-day bombardment, and General Winfield Scott began his march on Mexico City. Grant was among Scott's troops.

American troops storm the fiercely defended Mexican citadel of Chapultepec in early September 1847. Grant was with the shock troops — many of whom were U.S. marines — that finally captured the fortress.

As the citadel was taken, many of its teenage defenders committed suicide by hurling themselves from the high walls to the plain below. Then the assault on the city itself began. Grant was among the shock troops — many of them were U.S. marines — who fought their way into the city first. He saw a church belfry from which a well-placed cannon might fire upon the Mexican troops defending a crucial gate. Grant enlisted a few volunteers, took apart a howitzer, waded through water-filled ditches, and arrived at the front door of the church. Grant knocked at the door, and a Mexican priest answered and politely refused to let the Americans in. In his memoirs, Grant recalled the somewhat comical scene that followed: "With the little Spanish then at my command, I explained to him that he might save property by opening the door, and he certainly would save himself from becoming a prisoner, for a time at least; and besides, I intended to go in whether he consented or not. He began to see his duty in the same light I did, and opened the door, though he did not look as if it gave him special pleasure to do so." Grant and his men ran up the

stairs to the belfry, reassembled the cannon, and rained havoc on the Mexicans below.

That night, the Mexican general, Antonio Santa Anna, withdrew from the city with his entire army. Mexico City was in American hands. Grant was formally complimented for his actions during the assault and promoted to first lieutenant. Among the other officers to perform with distinction were John C. Pemberton, George B. McClellen, Pierre G. T. Beauregard, and Robert E. Lee — men Grant would become more closely acquainted with, in one way or another, in the years to come.

The American troops stayed in Mexico while efforts to establish a peace treaty dragged on. Grant used his leisure time to travel around the Valley of Mexico and write to Julia. The young man from Ohio fell in love with the country he had helped to subdue. He learned enough Spanish to talk to local villagers, hiked up Popocatepetl, an extinct volcano, with his friend Simon Buckner, and saw a bullfight. The kindness of the Mexican people and the magnificence of the scenery delighted him. The poverty of the masses and the brutality of the bullfight hor-

The triumphant army of General Winfield Scott enters Mexico City, September 14, 1847. Grant performed heroically throughout the Mexican War and was promoted to first lieutenant after the fall of Mexico City.

rified him. Finally, in February 1848, the Treaty of Guadalupe Hidalgo was signed. Mexico had no choice but to surrender its claims to Texas and the present states of California, New Mexico, Utah, Nevada, Arizona, and Colorado — for $15 million. The victorious American troops prepared to return home.

The Mexican War left a deep and long-lasting impression on Grant. The two generals he served under in Mexico, Scott and Taylor, influenced him more than any other individuals he encountered, or would encounter, in his lifetime. Grant had studied both men closely throughout the war. Zachary Taylor, known affectionately as Old Rough and Ready to his troops, provided Grant with the foundation for the style of leadership he would assume years later in the Civil War. He described the Zachary Taylor of the Mexican War in his memoirs: "General Taylor never made any great show or parade, either of uniform or retinue. In dress he was possibly too plain, rarely wearing anything in the field to indicate his rank, or even that he was an officer; but he was known to every soldier in his army, and was respected by all. Taylor was not a conversationalist, but on paper he could put his meaning so clearly that there could be no mistaking it. No soldier could face either danger or responsibility more calmly than he." Grant's great admiration for Taylor is evident. His description of his former commander is also striking because it could easily pass for a description of Grant himself as a commander in the Civil War.

Grant was influenced by General Scott in a different way. Scott, known (not so affectionately) as Old Fuss and Feathers to his men, affected a leadership style that was the opposite of Taylor's, a style that Grant disdained: "He always wore all the uniform prescribed or allowed by law when he inspected his lines; word would be sent to all divisions and brigade commanders in advance, notifying them of the hour when the commanding general might be expected. This was done so that all the army might be under arms to salute their chief as he passed." Although Grant disliked Scott's flamboyance, he had nothing but respect and admiration for the tactical sense that the general displayed during the Mexican campaign. Scott moved quickly, struck first, seized the initiative. He was undaunted by the size of his enemy's army and had a creative knack for turning adverse situations — such as the rough terrain at Cerro Gordo — to his own advantage. Grant took note of these elements and stored them away for later use.

It was a much different Ulysses Grant who returned to White Haven to lay claim to Julia Dent in August 1848. The new Grant, at 26, carried himself with the self-assurance of a man who knows he has performed well in the most trying of situations — war. He was handsome, healthy, and confident, full of optimism and ambition, and if Julia still harbored any doubts about him, they were swept away within minutes of his return. Her parents were only too happy to see their daughter matched with the impressive young lieutenant. As they set sail down the Mississippi River on their honeymoon cruise, the future seemed bright with promise, and Ulysses and Julia had only great expectations. They could not have suspected that around the next bend lay hardship, doubt, failure, and poverty.

3

"Poverty, Poverty"

Although Grant still entertained plans to become a math teacher, after his marriage to Julia he decided to remain in the army. This decision was perhaps the first indication that Grant was less than confident about his prospects as a civilian. Although his salary as a quartermaster would be inadequate for supporting a growing family, and although he would discover that he hated the peacetime army, Grant opted for the relative security of the military rather than the uncertainty of civilian life. He had been in West Point and then the army since the age of 17, and to him the world outside the military was an unknown quantity.

> *His gullibility was exceeded only by his bad luck.*
> —WILLIAM S. McFEELY
> historian, on Grant's lack of business acumen

It was a young, confident, and ambitious Ulysses S. Grant who returned from the Mexican War to marry his sweetheart, Julia Dent, in the summer of 1848. Neither Julia nor Ulysses could have foreseen the difficult and painful days that lay ahead.

Things went alright initially. Grant's regiment was posted to Sackets Harbor, on Lake Ontario in upstate New York, and they arrived there in the fall of 1848. Ulysses was passionately in love, and he doted on his bride. His quartermaster's duties were not difficult, and he focused his attention on enjoying the company of his wife and the new friends they made. He loved to sit quietly, smoke cigars, and play checkers. Julia, however, was not quite so content. Life at Sackets Harbor was nothing like what she had known at White Haven. She had dreamed of living in a great house with many servants. Julia was a resilient woman, however; she loved her husband deeply and made the best of what life at an army post had to offer. On May 20, 1850, she gave birth to Frederick Dent Grant. Ulysses was overjoyed.

Prospectors take a break from their labors and pose for a photograph during the California gold rush of 1849. Grant was among the soldiers who were sent to the West Coast to keep order in those unruly times.

The Grants' long, agonizing slide into near destitution began, ironically, with the discovery of gold on the West Coast. As the gold rush intensified and hundreds of thousands of people flocked to California to make their fortunes, it became clear that troops would have to be sent to the coast to keep the peace. In the spring of 1852, Grant's unit was ordered west; they would travel to California via the Isthmus of Panama. But Julia was pregnant again, and Grant knew that exposing her to the hardships of such a journey during the malarial summer months was out of the question. Grant considered resigning his commission but concluded that with all the new wealth circulating on the Pacific Coast he should be able to supplement his quartermaster's pay with enough money to allow him to eventually send for his family. So, in the spring of 1852, Julia and Fred were sent to live with Grant's parents, who had moved to Bethel, Ohio, and Ulysses boarded a steamer for Panama.

Julia gave birth to Ulysses S. Grant, Jr., in July. Her husband spent most of that month engaged in a nightmarish passage across the Isthmus of Panama. Grant displayed good judgment in leaving his wife behind: One-third of those who attempted the journey died of yellow fever, malaria, cholera, or dysentery. For many of those who made the journey, Ulysses Grant proved to be something of a hero. As quartermaster, he was in charge of travel arrangements. When the company of troops and their dependents became stranded on the Atlantic coast of Panama because the mules they had contracted for were not delivered, Grant first calmed the travelers' growing panic and then went into a nearby marketplace and paid much more than his orders authorized to secure enough mules and porters to get his people moving through the jungle to the Pacific Ocean. Those who survived the crossing of Panama never forgot the reserves of quiet strength and resourcefulness that Grant displayed in averting disaster for the group. The Little Man of Iron, as they fondly called him, slept only a few hours a night and spent most of his time tending to the sick, dealing with hostile natives, soothing women and children, and comforting dying men.

Grant arrived in San Francisco only to learn that he had been reassigned to the Columbia Barracks, at Fort Vancouver in Oregon. He arrived there in late 1852. It was not long before he began to pine for his wife and children. The spectacular, mountainous scenery that surrounded the tiny, crudely constructed army post only made him feel lonely and insignificant. There was very little to do except to observe the Indians, greet occasional wagon trains filled with new settlers, and wait for the sporadic and undependable mail. Knowing that he would never be able to support a growing family on his meager army pay, Grant began casting about for a way to make more money. "There is no reason why an active, energetic person should not make a fortune every year," Grant assured his wife in a letter, but his seeming confidence masked a growing desperation. One after another, his forays into the world of business failed miserably.

First, a man named Elijah Camp, whom Grant had known at Sackets Harbor, talked Grant into investing the pay he had accumulated during the trip west in a store that Camp was establishing in San Francisco. The store failed and Grant lost every cent of his investment. He saved his pay again. When they heard that the people of San Francisco were desperate for ice, Grant and some fellow officers pooled their money, purchased a large shipment, and sent it to San Francisco, only to discover that a huge shipload had arrived in the city just a few days before. Their ice melted unsold. Grant tried again; this time, he grew potatoes, hoping to sell them to the hordes of hungry immigrants arriving daily on the West Coast; unfortunately, everyone else seemed to have had the same idea at the same time. The effect of so many people trying to sell their produce at once was not conducive to profit making. Once again, Grant lost money.

As the likelihood of ever making enough money to bring Julia and his sons to the West became increasingly slim, Grant became depressed. He sat alone for hours, glumly reading and rereading his wife's letters. "He seemed," said a sergeant who lived with him, "to be always sad." In February 1854,

Grant was transferred to remote Fort Humboldt on the northern California coast. The few friends he did have were left behind. His despair deepened. In a letter to Julia, he wrote, "Poverty, poverty, begins to stare me in the face. You do not know how forsaken I feel here." Awash in loneliness and self-pity, Grant started to drink.

Stories of Grant's drinking problem have reached mythical proportions through the years. The idea of an unshaven, wild-eyed, whiskey-crazed Grant leading the Union army during the Civil War has become part of the Grant legend. In truth, however, he drank only in certain situations. Despite his seemingly solitary nature as a boy, as a man (he was now 31), Grant became increasingly dependent on the companionship of his wife. He needed her with him to feel whole. At Humboldt, her absence, combined with the endless boredom and inactivity of day-to-day life in a peacetime army, helped to undermine any self-sufficiency that remained. Along with loneliness, boredom and waiting could completely unnerve the man. Grant was fine as long as he had something meaningful to do. Later, during the Civil War, Grant drank also, occasionally — but never during battle. It was only during the long, anxiety-laden hours in between combat that he succumbed to drink. Had there been a battle to fight 365 days a year, Grant would have remained as sober as a judge.

San Francisco was a wild boomtown during the 1850s, filled with men who had come west to seek their fortune. Most of them failed terribly and ended up with little to their name.

So, Grant drank. Many times a day he could be seen at the local trading post whiskey barrel, filling his tin cup. Soon, he had developed a reputation as an alcoholic. Finally, after Grant had reported for duty drunk once too often, his commanding officer had Grant write out an unsigned resignation. He warned Grant that the next time he was unable to fulfill his duties because of drinking, his military career would be over. Predictably, his military career soon ended — for the time being, at least. Grant's superiors offered him a choice: He could sign his resignation or face a court-martial. Grant signed.

Discharged, Grant went to San Francisco, rented a small room, and spent all his remaining money on liquor. He felt worthless, like just another hopeless drunk in a city filled with hopeless drunks, men who had come west dreaming of gold and had found only poverty and despair. In fact, Grant soon became indistinguishable from such people. Acquaintances who did happen to recognize him were shocked at his appearance, and Grant avoided them whenever

Grant was proud of "Hardscrabble," the house that he built during his abortive attempt at farming, but his wife hated it. The house was the only thing Grant had ever built with his own hands.

he could. Fortunately, one of his friends would not be put off, and Grant was provided with a ticket back east. He departed for home in the summer of 1854. He was no doubt happy at the prospect of being reunited with his wife and two sons — one son he had yet to lay eyes on — but he must have dreaded it as well. It would not be like his homecoming after the Mexican War.

Despite the less than favorable conditions under which he returned, the mere fact that he was together with his family again helped Grant to shake off his depression and shame. He had learned a valuable lesson, and never again would he allow himself to be separated from Julia for more than a month or two at a time. Sure that the worst was behind him, Grant stopped drinking and set about building a new life for himself and his family. Julia had been given 60 acres of farmland outside St. Louis as a wedding present from her father. Grant decided to move onto the land and become a farmer. His father gave him enough money to buy livestock and seed, and his father-in-law loaned him money to start building a house. In the meantime, the Grants lived in a house that belonged to one of Julia's brothers, and Grant chopped and sold wood for a living. He became a familiar sight on a certain St. Louis street corner, standing next to a pile of wood, still wearing his old army overcoat.

After he had dug the foundation and prepared the lumber himself, neighbors helped Grant put up his new house. He was proud of the rough, ramshackle structure, and he named it Hardscrabble. Julia was dismayed at the crude dwelling that Grant expected her to live in, but she said nothing. She was pregnant again, and gave birth to their first girl, Nellie, at Hardscrabble in 1856. In the meantime, Grant's farming efforts began to falter. He was no businessman, and it soon became evident that he was no farmer either. Although he worked hard, the farm never succeeded. He had to keep asking Jesse Grant for money and accepting charity from Frederick Dent. Once again, Ulysses Grant was faced with the prospect of failure. Depression set in. His shoulders became stooped, his face drawn. He looked older than he was. Dressed in muddy boots,

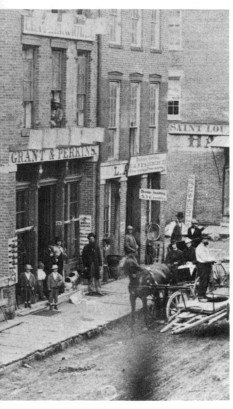

Grant & Perkins leather-goods store in Galena, Illinois, where Grant spent the dismal years preceding the Civil War, "ready," in the words of F. Scott Fitzgerald, "to be called to an intricate destiny."

oversized pants, and a shabby, old flannel shirt, Grant presented a sorry sight indeed. When an army friend stopped to ask a disheveled, bearded laborer where he might find Ulysses Grant, he was appalled to discover that it was Grant he was addressing. "Good God," he gasped. Grant replied to the man's queries with bitter sarcasm: "I am solving the problem of poverty."

Grant slipped further into debt, and his depression began to manifest itself in physical symptoms. Fever, chills, loss of appetite and energy, and a general, numbing listlessness set in. Hardscrabble was abandoned in 1858, the same year his fourth and final child, Jesse, was born. His farm implements were auctioned off. Julia and the children moved back to White Haven. Grant went to St. Louis, where Fred Dent had secured him a position as a real estate sales agent and rent collector. Grant was not cut out for the work. He hated trying to get people to buy property almost as much as he despised trying to force impoverished tenants to pay their overdue rent. Every Saturday that winter, too poor to afford a horse, he walked the 12 miles out to White Haven to spend the weekend with Julia and the children.

By the spring of 1860, Ulysses Grant seemed a beaten man. He had failed at everything he tried and could secure no more "loans" from anyone in St. Louis. Now he sat quietly by himself for hours. He was 37, he had a wife and 4 children, no money, no job, and no prospects. There was nothing left to do but swallow his pride and beg his father to give him work — a fate Grant had dreaded ever since his return from the West. The journey to his father's house was an agony to Grant, the low point of his life. He thought about the first business transaction he had ever made, so long ago, when he had failed, as an eight year old, to bargain successfully for a colt. Nothing had changed. The humiliation that his self-righteous, pedantic father was sure to subject him to would be unbearable.

To his credit, Jesse Grant inflicted no more pain on his son. It was obvious to him that Ulysses had suffered enough. Jesse took one look at his firstborn and accepted that he would have to take care of him — Ulysses obviously could not manage on his own. Jesse Grant had set Ulysses' brother up in a successful leather goods store in Galena, Illinois. Ulysses could work for them as a clerk at a salary of $600 a year. He had not earned $60 a year as a farmer. Ulysses was grateful and relieved. He moved his family into a little brick house in Galena. The house bordered a cemetery.

Grant no longer had to worry about where his children's next meal would come from. He finally had a measure of security. He was a clerk. He diligently reported to work every morning, tied on his apron, and did his job. But he was clearly an unhappy, spiritless man. Julia watched him in the morning and when he came home from work in the evening and wondered what had happened to her brave young lieutenant. He took interest in only two things — his children and the newspapers. He only seemed truly alive when he was playing with his four kids. His peculiar naïveté, a liability in the adult world, was an asset in the world of children. Grant understood children and they understood him. There was a mutual trust. He could communicate with them on their own level. Every night before dinner, three-year-old Jesse would ask, "Hey mister, do you want to fight?" Grant would reply, "I am a man of peace, but I will not be hectored by a person of your size." Then they would wrestle on the floor until their food was ready.

Grant's only other interest during this period of brooding and silence was the newspapers. Each day he bought every paper he could and scoured them with intense concentration. It was clear to him that war was coming. Maybe a big war. So Grant the clerk put in his hours at the store, ate his meals, slept, played with his children, read the papers, and, as harsh as it may sound, he hoped. For the United States as a whole, the fateful events of 1860–61 — the election of Abraham Lincoln, the secession of the Southern states from the Union, the shelling of Fort Sumter — signaled the beginning of a calamity of unprecedented scope. For Ulysses S. Grant, however, they signaled redemption.

I saw new energies in Grant. He dropped a stoop shouldered way of walking, and set his hat foreward on his forehead in a careless fashion.
—JOHN A. RAWLINS
a neighbor of Grant's in Galena, on his change of disposition with the coming of the war

4

The Hornets' Nest

Many Americans were faced with a painful decision following the outbreak of the Civil War. For others, the decision was easy. Grant was among the latter group. His loyalties lay entirely with the Union. He did not like slavery, but he had never been an abolitionist; in fact, he had owned a slave himself once, during his abortive attempt at farming in Missouri, but he set the man free before long. A total and immediate abolition of slavery in the states seemed politically and socially unfeasible to Grant; he felt that a program of gradual emancipation with compensation to the slaveholders was called for. But from the beginning he was against the expansion of slavery into the new territories such as Kansas and Texas.

I feel great confidence in ultimately reducing the place.
—ULYSSES S. GRANT
in a letter to General Halleck concerning Fort Donelson

The Union Army of the Potomac encamped at Cumberland Landing, Maryland. Following the bombing of Fort Sumter in April 1861, Northerners responded with enthusiasm to President Lincoln's call for volunteers, and Grant found himself in command of a federal army.

Up until the bombing of the federal garrison at Fort Sumter by Confederate artillery, Grant had felt there was room for compromise with the South. But for him, and many other Americans, the concept of the *Union* had an almost holy significance. Grant felt that when the Southern states seceded and then engaged in a hostile act against the United States government, they forced the issue to a point of no return. Secession was an act of treason, as far as he was concerned, and in undertaking this act, the Southerners had staked "their lives, their property, and every claim for protection given by citizenship — on the issue. Victory, or the conditions imposed by the conqueror — must be the result." Ulysses Grant was for the Union, and he would fight to preserve it, if they would let him.

Grant himself never seemed to have had any doubt that he would be reinstated into the army. On the day that Union volunteers were being mustered in Galena, Grant left the leather shop to go see what was happening, and he never returned. His fall from grace in the U.S. Army had been agonizingly slow; his resurrection was meteoric. The Union was desperate for trained officers to lead the hordes of men who were responding to President Lincoln's call for volunteers. Grant made himself useful and visible at the recruiting center. With the help of Elihu B. Washburne, an Illinois congressman who took a liking to Grant, and despite the continued whisperings about his drinking problem, by June 1861, Colonel Ulysses S. Grant was leading the Twenty-First Illinois Regiment into Missouri.

In August, having seen no combat as yet, and again with the help of Washburne, Grant was promoted to brigadier general. He began gathering a staff about him. As a general, he would need a group of men he could depend on and trust. John A. Rawlins, a handsome, intense young attorney from Galena, was brought in. William S. Hillyer, a real estate agent Grant knew from St. Louis, joined the staff, as did William R. Rowley, another Galena neighbor, Adam Badeau, Horace Porter, Cyrus B. Comstock, and Orville E. Babcock. Most of these men would remain with Grant, in one capacity or another, throughout the war and after.

Brigadier General John Aaron Rawlins, a neighbor of Grant's from Galena, was one of Grant's first aides-de-camp. According to Grant, Rawlins was "indispensable" to him.

Grant was back in his own element. He was in a war, and to him, war was simple: Find the enemy and destroy him. Grant set about doing this immediately. His force had crossed the Mississippi and come to rest at Cairo, Illinois, a location that gave Grant access to the Mississippi, Ohio, Tennessee, and Cumberland rivers. They were now in what would come to be known as the western theater of war, where rivers were of the utmost strategic importance. The key river was the Mississippi, the nation's main artery and the lifeline of the South; it was in Confederate hands as far north as Memphis, Tennessee. Two other important rivers connecting the North and the South were the Cumberland and the Tennessee. Both passed close to Cairo and were controlled by two Confederate forts, Donelson and Henry, in Tennessee.

Grant (standing at center, on steps, with his right hand in his pocket) at his headquarters below the post office at Cairo, Illinois, in September 1861. From Cairo, Grant's army invaded the Tennessee River valley.

Grant moved first up the Ohio River, occupying Paducah, Kentucky, which gave him access to the Tennessee River. On November 6, under orders to make a "demonstration" against the enemy, he crammed 3,000 troops onto Union navy gunboats, which carried them 20 miles down the Mississippi River to the Confederate outpost at Belmont, Missouri. At dawn on November 7, Grant led his men ashore and they attacked Belmont. This was Grant's idea of a demonstration. A sharp, two-hour battle ensued, during which Grant had a horse shot out from under him. Although this was the first combat experience for many of Grant's men, they fought well and hard, and the Confederates, under General Gideon J. Pillow, were forced to abandon their encampment.

At this point, the Union troops showed their inexperience, breaking ranks and looting the camp. In the meantime, Confederate general Leonidas Polk, who held the town of Columbus, Kentucky, across the river from Belmont, was crossing the river to reinforce Pillow. Grant faced his first crisis of the war. He got the attention of his overexcited troops by setting the Confederate tents on fire. He pointed out that steamers filled with Confederate reinforcements were closing in on them and that, in the other direction, the rebels they had driven from camp were re-forming and preparing to counterattack. Grant and his men were on the verge of being surrounded. Some of his new officers suggested surrender. Grant calmly replied that they had fought their way in and would fight their way out if they had to. The men re-formed their ranks and began to move as quickly as possible back onto their boats. To make sure that the Confederates coming ashore did not realize how disorganized his men were in their retreat, Grant sat calmly upon his horse, smoking a cigar in full view of the advancing enemy, until all his men were on board and the boats were ready to leave. Although he was forced to retreat, the raid on Belmont proved to be a psychological victory for Grant, not so much over the enemy, but rather, over his own men. After Belmont, the soldiers under Grant saw him in a new light. He was a man they would fight for.

Back in Cairo, Grant's men licked their wounds and contemplated their first taste of war. Their commander was already planning his next move: Grant had his sights set on Forts Henry and Donelson. He believed he could take them both. He went to St. Louis to propose this action to his superior, General Henry W. Halleck. Halleck did not like Grant; he had heard the stories about Grant's drinking, and he disapproved of Grant's proletarian style of army dress. He rejected Grant's plan. Grant was undeterred, however; he returned to Cairo and conferred with navy flag officer Andrew H. Foote. Foote liked Grant, and he liked Grant's plan. He resubmitted Grant's proposal to Halleck under the guise of a naval operation. This time, Halleck approved. On February 3, 1862, 7 gunboats under Foote's command escorted a fleet of transport ships, bristling with 17,000 Union troops under Grant, up the Tennessee River to Fort Henry. On February 6, under heavy bombardment from Foote's gunboats, Fort Henry fell. Grant's army suffered only one casualty.

Grant wanted Fort Donelson, too. On the bitter winter night of February 14, he marched his army the 13 miles to where Donelson stood guard over the Cumberland River. Again, with support from Foote's gunboats, an assault was launched. But Donelson was much more heavily fortified than Henry, and the thousands of Confederates within put up a fierce fight. After inflicting heavy damage on the fort, Foote's gunboats were hit with artillery shells and rendered useless. The federal troops watched the lifeless, smoking gunboats as they were carried off by the river. The rebels inside the fort cheered wildly at the sight. Grant ordered his men to dig in. Soon, the fort was ringed by the entrenched Union army. Night fell, and the exchange of artillery and rifle fire became sporadic and then died off altogether. Grant lit a cigar and set off on his horse to locate Foote.

At dawn on the morning of February 15, while Grant was downriver conferring with Foote (who had been badly wounded the day before), the Confederates attacked. They concentrated the assault at a specific point in the Union lines, hoping to break through the siege circle to a road that would take them toward Nashville and safety. The Union troops were taken completely by surprise, and they were on the verge of breaking when Grant returned to the scene. He found his officers in a state of confusion and his soldiers in a demoralized condition. The fighting was bitter, for the Southerners were desperate, and they had driven the Union troops back onto the road that led to Nashville. Two simple but steely orders from Grant remedied the situation. To his officers, he said, "Gentlemen, that road must be recovered before night." Then, riding up and down the lines, he told his troops that "the enemy is trying to escape and he must not be permitted to do so." A counterattack was launched, the Union forces rallied, and the enemy was forced to retreat back into the fort. There were heavy casualties on both sides.

For the rebel troops, the situation was now hopeless. They had been badly mauled in their attempt to break out, the fort was surrounded, and Union

reinforcements were arriving by the hour. The commander of the fort, General Simon Bolivar Buckner, an old friend of Grant's from the Mexico days, saw no choice but to surrender. During the predawn hours of February 16, Grant received a message from Buckner requesting a truce so that "terms of capitulation" could be discussed. Grant's reply became the most famous communiqué in the history of American warfare: "Sir, Yours of this date proposing armistice and appointment of Commissioners to settle terms of capitulation, is just received. No terms except an unconditional and immediate surrender can be accepted. I propose to move immediately upon your works. Your obedient servant, U. S. Grant."

Union and Confederate troops clash outside Fort Donelson, Tennessee, in February 1862. Grant's bold assault on the rebel stronghold captured the attention of the people of the North — including President Lincoln.

General Simon Bolivar Buckner, an old friend of Grant's from West Point and the Mexican War, was in command of Fort Donelson when it was besieged by Grant. It was Buckner who received Grant's demand for an "unconditional surrender" of the fort.

Buckner surrendered Fort Donelson and 12,000 troops — unconditionally — and the North, up to this point starved for meaningful victories, had a new hero: Unconditional Surrender Grant. He was promoted to major general and given command of the Army of the Tennessee, but he scarcely stopped to acknowledge the fact. While General Halleck, jealous over the publicity Grant had received after Donelson, attempted to undermine Grant's authority by spreading rumors about his alleged drinking, Grant himself pressed eastward through Tennessee. Halleck's attempts at character assassination failed; President Lincoln, exasperated with inept and timid generals, gave Grant a vote of confidence. "I cannot spare this man," Lincoln said of Grant. "He fights." Grant kept to his policy of search and destroy; he was now focused on Corinth, Mississippi, where a massive Confederate army was encamped under the command of the highly regarded General Albert Sidney Johnston of Texas.

Aside from the soon-to-be-legendary Robert E. Lee and Stonewall Jackson, Johnston was reputed to be the most formidable commander fighting under the Confederate banner, and up to this point in the war, the Southern generals, for the most part, had been soundly whipping their Northern counterparts, giving credence to the widely held belief that the Southern man was naturally superior to the Northerner where military matters were concerned. But Grant was not impressed by the reputations of his Southern foes, and he would scoff at their supposed military brilliance throughout the war and, indeed, until his dying day. To him, they were mere mortals, like himself, and therefore he would treat them as such.

Grant moved inexorably toward Corinth and Johnston, heading straight for the largest concentration of enemy troops he could find and absorbing regiments and divisions of other Union armies as he went. Johnston knew that Grant was coming, and reinforcements flooded into his camp as well. By the time Grant's Army of the Tennessee arrived at Pittsburg Landing, Tennessee, just east of Corinth, it had swollen to 42,000 men, and Grant was expecting General Don Carlos Buell's Army of the Ohio, numbering 20,000, to arrive shortly. Johnston, with an army of 40,000, was within striking distance. The two great swarms of men blanketed the countryside on the western side of the Tennessee River. Restlessly aware of one another, the Northerners and Southerners settled into camp as dusk approached on April 5. Night fell, and the rolling landscape was dotted with campfires in all directions, as far as the eye could see. Grant set off on a boat for Savannah, 12 miles downriver, to confer with Buell, who had arrived there ahead of his troops.

Grant was eating his breakfast in Savannah the next morning at about six o'clock when he heard the tremendous racket of gunfire drifting down the river and realized he had made his first mistake of the war. It was a big mistake. Overconfident after his successes at Fort Donelson and Fort Henry, Grant never seriously considered the possibility

Although many of his fellow commanders disapproved of Grant, President Lincoln admired his style. Despite persistent rumors of alcohol abuse, Lincoln refused to dismiss Grant. "I can't spare this man," the president said. "He fights."

Albert Sidney Johnston was in command of the 40,000 Confederate troops encamped at Pittsburg Landing, Tennessee, in the spring of 1862. On April 6, the rebels attacked Grant's army, and the Battle of Shiloh began. Johnston did not survive the day.

that the enemy might attack him first. He fully expected them to entrench themselves and make the Union troops come in after them. Subsequently, he failed to post sufficient pickets (lookouts) around the perimeter of his encampment. When the sun came up on the morning of April 6, thousands of Confederate soldiers came with it, screaming and howling across the fields and out of the woods with fixed bayonets. Federal troops, still groggy with sleep, were slaughtered as they crouched around campfires preparing breakfast. Many were impaled on Southern bayonets as they struggled into their uniforms or desperately tried to load their flintlocks. Some never made it out of their sleeping rolls. The majority simply ran. As Grant made the torturously slow trip back upriver, his Army of the Tennessee was in grave danger of being broken completely.

Grant arrived at the battlefield at about nine o'clock that morning. He was greeted by a scene of absolute chaos. His army was in trouble, although they were not yet in a state of total retreat. Because of the actions of a certain few commanders, most notably General William Tecumseh Sherman and General Benjamin M. Prentiss, the Union lines had somehow held. They were being driven inexorably back toward the river, and gaping holes had been punched in the lines, but they had not crumbled completely. The situation, however, was grim. If there was ever a time for Grant to panic, this was it. But Grant did not panic, although he seemed quite annoyed. He went in search of his generals and started giving orders.

The Union defense slowly stiffened and their lines began to reassume a semblance of order. Johnston's men kept coming, thousands upon thousands of them. A huge and terrible battle took shape, raging across miles of Tennessee countryside. To that point, it was the largest battle ever fought on the North American continent. Some of the hardest fighting in a war that would become renowned for the ferocity of its combat took place during the next eight hours. In certain areas, confrontations of a harrowing intensity developed; these grim sites were given their own names. There was the Bloody

Pond, clogged with dead men by noon, its water turned crimson; there was the Peach Orchard, where the ceaseless firing brought an incongruously delicate shower of spring petals down on the hundreds of dead and dying and on those who stood among them and fought; and perhaps worst of all, near old Shiloh Church, there was the Hornets' Nest, so named because the air was angrily alive with buzzing musket balls and hissing shot and shrapnel. The area around Shiloh Church was at the center of the federal line; it had to be held at all costs. There, in the Hornets' Nest, Prentiss and his men fought for hours in the teeth of what one survivor called a "pitiless storm of leaden hail." Finally, when there were too few of them left to fight, they were captured, but their desperate holding action in the Hornets' Nest kept the Union center intact and probably averted a complete rout.

As the afternoon wore on, the rebel offensive began to lose its momentum. The sun was obscured by the thick clouds of smoke and the two armies fought in a kind of premature dusk. The Union troops were no longer falling back. General Sherman was everywhere at once, it seemed, although two horses were shot out from under him and he was hit by two bullets himself. And Grant began to appear. His plain uniform, the ever-present cigar, his cavalryman's hat, and the relaxed, slouching way he sat his horse were already well known to his troops, and a glimpse of him through the smoke was enough to rally a dispirited regiment. A young Union volunteer from Illinois who fought in and around the Hornets' Nest that day described how he looked up from his hiding place behind a fallen tree to see the general: "He went by us at a gallop. . . . Shot and shell were whizzing overhead, and cutting off the limbs of trees, but Grant rode through the storm with perfect indifference, paying no more attention to the missiles than if they had been paper wads." Grant's calm demeanor worked like a talisman on the demoralized federals. Many of the men who had fled to the rear in terror now began to come forward to plug the holes in the Union lines. The rebel advance stalled.

Union brigadier general Benjamin M. Prentiss, one of the heroes of Shiloh. Prentiss and his men fought in the deadly Hornets' Nest; their desperate stand during the morning of April 6 kept the federal lines from collapsing altogether.

Grant leads the charge that finally broke the Confederates during the second day of the bloody Battle of Shiloh. "Oh God forever keep me out of such another fight," a rebel soldier wrote.

The fighting died down as night approached. Darkness fell on a scene of appalling carnage. As he rode back to his command center, Grant saw "an open field over which the Confederates had made repeated charges, so covered with dead that it would have been possible to walk across the clearing, in any direction, stepping on dead bodies, without a foot touching the ground." On the previous night the landscape had been blanketed with the living; now it was covered with the dead and dying. Soon the temperature dropped and a cold rain began to fall. It rained all night long.

Clearly, the Confederates had carried the day. The federals had been driven back more than a mile. But Grant, who spent the night sitting under a tree in the rain, unable to sleep, was confident. His army had been bent, but not broken. Buell had arrived with his 20,000 men, General Lew Wallace had brought more reinforcements, and Union gunboats had come up the river. At dawn, Grant would return the favor and attack first. For the rebels, it was a hellish night. They felt that victory had been snatched from their grasp, and they were dismayed

by what one rebel called the "infernally stubborn" resistance the federals had put up. Worst of all, word was spreading that General Johnston had been killed. The Southerners shivered in the freezing spring rain and tried to sleep, but Grant had ordered the gunboats to lob a shell into their midst every 15 minutes, and they were almost glad to see the dawn when it came, although they knew what it would bring.

By the end of the second day, Grant's massive, vicious counteroffensive had broken the Confederates' will, and they had been driven from the field in full retreat. The Battle of Shiloh was over. Although it was inconclusive in traditional military terms, Shiloh was a watershed event in the Civil War. Two days of fighting had left 23,000 casualties, including almost 4,000 dead. Both sides now realized that their enemy was serious; both sides now knew that a quick, decisive victory was impossible. The dogs of war had been set loose, and in the North and the South, citizens and soldiers prepared themselves for the grueling struggle to come. After Shiloh, there was no turning back.

5

The Guns of Vicksburg

On June 6, 1862, the city of Memphis, Tennessee, was invaded by federal troops following a spectacular river battle. Civilians had lined the banks of the Mississippi early that morning to watch the fight between the ironclads of Union commodore Charles Davis and the gunboats of Confederate captain James E. Montgomery. By dusk, the rebel vessels had all been captured or sunk, and the people of Memphis, many of them weeping, returned to their homes to await the federal occupation troops. (Unlike the battle on land, the action on the rivers and the Atlantic was dominated by the federal navy throughout the war.) The Union now held the two ends of the Mississippi that lay within the theater of war — Memphis and New Orleans, which had been taken in April by the redoubtable Admiral David ("Damn the Torpedoes") Farragut. But between Memphis and New Orleans lay Vicksburg, whose heavy guns, perched on high bluffs overlooking the Mississippi, still ruled the river. To win complete control of the great waterway, the Union had to take Vicksburg.

He was in total control. One soldier who had been fighting on the hill watched Grant stand, "cool and calculating," with a cigar in his mouth ordering fresh assaults over bloody ground.
—WILLIAM S. McFEELY
historian, on Grant at the
Battle of Vicksburg

A disconsolate Grant sits outside his tent after being relieved of command of the Army of the Tennessee in the summer of 1862. He was reinstated in time to lead the campaign against the Confederate city of Vicksburg, Mississippi.

Grant spent the summer of 1862 trying to plan and organize a campaign against the city. There were several things that stood in his way. Vicksburg would be a hard nut to crack, first of all. It had been fortified to the teeth, and approaching it via the river seemed to be out of the question. But to march an army along the Mississippi and through the impenetrable swampland that surrounded Vicksburg would also be an extremely difficult task. These obstacles did not bother Grant, however; he felt that once he got started he would find a way to assail the Confederate stronghold. The problem was getting started.

It was not Confederate defenses or southern terrain that derailed Grant's drive down the Mississippi in the summer of 1862. Rather, it was political infighting and the professional jealousy of some of Grant's fellow officers. Ulysses Grant was a man who could remain unperturbed while thousands of enemy troops overran his lines at Shiloh, but he was also a man who was unnerved by the more petty battles of day-to-day life, such as bargaining for a horse or starting a business or running a farm. Now, bedeviled once again by General Halleck, Grant was unequipped to deal with his superior's disingenuous tactics. Halleck, who wanted direct control of the Army of the Tennessee and its impending drive on Vicksburg, managed to get Grant out of the way by promoting him to second in command of all the western armies, an administrative position. To Grant's utter horror, he found himself pushing papers rather than leading armies into combat. And because of his trusting nature, he did not realize or even suspect that his career had been sabotaged by a man who was supposedly a colleague and comrade-in-arms. The elusive origin of the problem made it all the more frustrating, and Grant seriously considered resigning.

Grant survived this crisis for two reasons. The first was that, unlike his dark period on the West Coast, he now had Julia and his children with him, and they provided him with the companionship and trust that were so necessary to his own sense of well-being. Second, Grant received the support of the men who had fought for him and who genuinely

You could not be quiet at home for a week when armies were moving.
—WILLIAM T. SHERMAN
in a letter to Grant,
June 1862

liked and admired him. General Sherman especially was instrumental in keeping Grant from doing something rash.

Sherman, one of the heroes of Shiloh, was a born warrior with a hawk's eyes, a red beard, and a terribly pitted face. An orphan who had been raised by an Ohio preacher (whose daughter he eventually married), Sherman possessed a keen intellect, a wry and sometimes dark sense of humor, and unbounded energy. He was fearless in combat and known for giving battlefield speeches of a Shakespearean eloquence. Sherman was as restless and talkative as Grant was composed and taciturn, and their differing personalities complemented one another. (The combination would eventually prove deadly to the Confederate cause.) Grant and Sherman had developed a strong friendship since Shiloh, and during the summer of 1862, hearing rumors that Grant might resign, Sherman sought out his friend and talked him out of it. Sherman had a far better understanding of army politics than Grant, and he assured his despairing friend that the best course of action was to sit tight and wait. Grant took Sherman's advice, Halleck was promoted to army chief of staff in July and departed to Washington, and Grant was back in command of the Army of the Tennessee. It is mind-boggling to consider what course the Civil War might have taken had Sherman not had his talk with Grant that summer.

With Halleck out of his hair and autumn approaching, Grant sat at his desk in his headquarters in La Grange, Mississippi, smoked cigars, and, in the words of poet Richard Wilbur, "chewed through scheme on scheme for toppling Vicksburg like a house of cards." Vicksburg, however, was no house of cards. On November 9, 1862, General Grant initiated his first campaign against the city, marching his army south to Holly Springs and dispatching Sherman, with 3 regiments, by boat up the Yazoo River to the point where it emptied into the Mississippi, 12 miles northwest of Vicksburg. Sherman was then to assault the heavily fortified Chickasaw Bluffs, which defended that approach to Vicksburg.

Federal commander William Tecumseh Sherman, known as "Uncle Billy" to his troops, was Grant's most able general; he participated in the Vicksburg campaign and was instrumental in breaking the Southern rebellion.

Fugitive negroes, fleeing the vengeful Confederate armies, ford the Rappahannock River in Virginia during the summer of 1862. The task of protecting the refugees in the Mississippi Delta fell to Grant's Army of the Tennessee.

In the meantime, Grant attempted to march his army overland to Vicksburg. By December 20, however, he was mired in the lush, overgrown swampland of Mississippi, and rebel guerrilla bands were playing havoc with the federal columns. On December 29, Sherman attacked Chickasaw Bluffs but was beaten back by the Confederate defenders. "Well," Sherman wrote in a letter to his wife, "we have been to Vicksburg and it was too much for us and we have backed out." The Army of the Tennessee was in the process of backing out also; encumbered with thousands of black refugees, Grant was in danger of being trapped deep in hostile territory. The general pulled his army out and moved it back to Memphis. The first Vicksburg campaign had failed.

Grant spent the winter in Memphis, smoking and scheming. By early 1863 he had become convinced that the key to unlocking Vicksburg was to somehow get past the city and attack it from the south, rather than the north, because all the city's defenses were oriented to an assault from the north. But how could Grant get an army — and all the unwieldy supplies that were needed to sustain it in enemy territory — past Vicksburg's guns? He thought he might be able to find a channel through the bayous that was deep and wide enough to sail his army down and that would lead off the Mississippi north of Vicksburg and empty back into the river south of the city. He plunged back into the swamplands with his army. The channel could not be found.

President Lincoln suggested that the army engineers simply dig their own channel, and Grant had no choice but to humor the commander in chief's wishes. Up to their armpits in the rain-swollen swamps, 4,000 men spent the spring digging, building dams, hacking away foliage, fending off snakes and alligators, and ducking rebel snipers. Grant watched with amusement, smoked constantly to keep the insects off, and waited for the spring flooding to recede.

In April, when the Mississippi's floodwaters had withdrawn sufficiently, Grant crossed to the western side of the river and marched his army through the muck toward Vicksburg, which lay on the eastern side. Concealed by the swarming vegetation, and marching out of range of the big guns, the troops succeeded in getting south of Vicksburg, but horses and supply wagons could not follow — they simply sank into the mire. Grant left his army and traveled back upriver to confer with Rear Admiral David Dixon Porter of the Union navy. Porter, a bold sort, suggested a daring plan: Taking his cue from Admiral Farragut's actions on the Mississippi earlier in the war, he proposed loading Grant's supplies onto barges, surrounding them with gunboats, running the gauntlet of Vicksburg's guns by night, and linking up with the Army of the Tennessee south of the city. This idea appealed to Grant immensely.

On the night of April 16, under cover of darkness, Porter attempted to run his 12 vessels past the Vicksburg guns. The Confederates were expecting him, and to provide enough light to shoot by, they torched the huge, stately mansions that lined the cliffs, and set fire to all the foliage and trees along the river as well; they also built large rafts, loaded them with kindling, set them aflame, and anchored them in midstream. The stretch of the river that passed below Vicksburg was soon bathed in a flickering light that could be seen for miles. A fantastic scene awaited Grant, who was aboard one of the transports, as they sailed round a bend in the river and the inferno came into view. "The sight," Grant recalled after the war, "was magnificent, but terrible." Undaunted, and to Grant's everlasting ap-

Admiral David Dixon Porter of the U.S. Navy. Porter and Grant devised a daring plan to transport Union troops and supplies past the Vicksburg artillery batteries in April 1863.

proval, Porter piloted his fleet straight into this fiery illumination. The rebel batteries boomed to life. Porter's gunboats returned the fire. The river boiled like a caldron as the shells rained down around the Union vessels. Although several of the vessels were hit, they all managed to emerge from the maelstrom south of the city and relatively intact. They put ashore at a place named Hard Times, Mississippi, and indeed, hard times had come to Vicksburg. On the night of April 30, Porter's fleet carried Grant's army, now fully supplied, to the east bank of the Mississippi. The Army of the Tennessee was now south and to the rear of Vicksburg. Grant prepared to move on the city.

General John C. Pemberton put his force of 20,000 rebels in between Vicksburg and Grant's oncoming army. They clashed on May 16, at Champion's Hill. Grant's troops were not about to be stopped now, and Pemberton's army, after a fierce battle, was forced to retreat. Grant pursued them to the walls of Vicksburg, where the Confederates turned to fight once again. They had constructed an elaborate labyrinth of breastworks, ditches, and tunnels surrounding the city, and the terrain bris-

In one of the most spectacular scenes of the war, Admiral Porter's gunboats and supply barges steam down the mighty Mississippi River through the gauntlet of Vicksburg's guns on the night of April 16, 1863.

tled with sharpened stakes, the 19th-century equivalent of barbed wire. The rebels swarmed into their entrenchments like ants, fixed their bayonets, and waited. On May 19, Grant sent his men charging into the teeth of the enemy breastworks, but they were thrown back with heavy losses. On May 22, the federals launched another attack. Again and again they charged across the jagged landscape, only to be sent reeling backward, sometimes after ferocious hand-to-hand combat. Finally, Grant called an end to the suicidal charges. He had not brought his army this far to see it broken apart on the very outskirts of Vicksburg. He ordered his troops to start digging their own entrenchments. Starvation would accomplish what men and muskets could not. The siege of Vicksburg had begun.

A section of the elaborate network of trenches, breastworks, and barricades that Grant's army encountered around the perimeter of Vicksburg. The general's attempts to take the city by storm were unsuccessful, and his army settled in for a siege.

General George Gordon Meade (standing at center with both hands in his pockets) and his staff, shortly after the titanic Battle of Gettysburg — fought on July 1, 2, and 3 of 1863 — in which the Union Army of the Potomac defeated Robert E. Lee's Army of Northern Virginia.

At many places the Union entrenchments were only yards from the rebel ditches. For the first week or two the Northerners and Southerners hurled insults and taunts at each other; this eventually gave way to good-natured joking, gossip, and friendly conversation. Inside the city, the people huddled in caves while Union gunboats on the Yazoo River lobbed mortars over the walls. Spring turned to sweltering summer, and starvation and disease slowly eroded the will of the besieged. Outside the walls, on the perimeter of the rebel defenses, Grant was not enjoying the situation either. He did not have the temperament for a siege, and he had not seen his wife and children for a month. Anxious and restless, he spent a good deal of his time drinking. Finally, on July 3, to the relief of everyone involved, Pemberton sent out a note requesting terms of surrender. On the Fourth of July, 1863, the stubborn city was Grant's, the Confederacy had been cut in half, and the Mississippi River was once more a part of the Union. "The Father of Waters," President Lincoln said on hearing the news, "again goes unvexed to the sea."

The fall of Vicksburg, coupled with the news of the defeat of Robert E. Lee's Army of Northern Virginia by General George Gordon Meade's Army of the Potomac at the epic Battle of Gettysburg, touched off wild celebrations in the North. Grant's name was on everybody's lips — including the president's. Lincoln was now positive that Grant was the man to crush the rebellion once and for all, and he put Grant in charge of all the armies of the West — the Army of the Tennessee, the Army of the Ohio, and the Army of the Cumberland. Grant had little time to reflect on this promotion, however, for he was immediately dispatched to Chattanooga, in the mountainous southeastern region of Tennessee. There, the federal Army of the Cumberland, under General William Starke Rosecrans, had been badly mauled by Confederate general Braxton Bragg's army at the Battle of Chickamauga in mid-September. Rosecrans now found himself cornered at the railroad town of Chattanooga, with mountains, the Tennessee River, and Bragg's army blocking any escape. Lincoln sent Grant to the scene, hoping he could bail out Rosecrans.

Grant arrived at Chattanooga in late October. He set out on horseback just after dawn to assess the situation. The rebel troops on one riverbank watched as Grant rode at an easy canter down the other side. They recognized him — every soldier in the war knew of Grant by now and had heard what he looked like or seen pictures — and although he was well within range of their guns, no shots were fired. Instead, the Southerners casually saluted the general as he passed. Grant returned the salutes in an appropriately offhand manner and rode on.

Any general of any army would have found the situation of the Union troops at Chattanooga to be hopeless — except for Ulysses S. Grant. Indeed, when Sherman arrived with reinforcements, he declared, somewhat gleefully, "Why General Grant, you are besieged!" Grant did not see it that way. For him, "besieged" was a relative term — an army on the offensive was never besieged. He established his headquarters in a small house in Chattanooga,

> *Vicksburg was to be starved out. And while this ugly logic was being worked, Ulysses Grant got drunk.*
> —WILLIAM S. McFEELY
> historian, on Grant during
> the siege of Vicksburg

General Grant (left) confers with members of his staff on Lookout Mountain, Tennessee, in the autumn of 1863. He was in the process of breaking Confederate general Braxton Bragg's grip on Chattanooga.

ensconced himself before the fireplace, and began writing a seemingly endless succession of typically simple, straightforward orders. Messengers came and went constantly. The blizzard of small scraps of paper continued for a month, and Bragg watched in bewilderment as Union activity sprang up all over Tennessee. Union reinforcements converged on the area from all directions, fresh Union supply lines began to snake through passes in the mountains, pontoon bridges appeared suddenly over streams and the river. On November 23, Grant attacked. His generals — Sherman, Fighting Joe Hooker, George ("the Rock of Chickamauga") Thomas, and young, hell-bent cavalry commander Philip H. Sheridan — hit Bragg's troops in a multipronged offensive that included the battles of Chattanooga, Lookout Mountain, and Missionary Ridge. By November 26,

Bragg's siege was shattered and his army was on the run, with the merciless Sheridan in hot pursuit.

Grant's brilliant performance at Chattanooga had widespread ramifications. For the South, it was a catastrophe. In a letter to Confederate president Jefferson Davis, Braxton Bragg wrote, quite correctly, that the "disaster admits of no palliation." For the North, it was a decisive victory. "This is one of the most important gains of the war," Lincoln observed. Now the way to Georgia and the Deep South lay open to a Union invasion. And for Grant, Chattanooga was the pivotal event of his career. He was now recognized as the top general in the North; finally, someone had emerged to challenge Robert E. Lee. The obvious differences between the two appealed to the people of the North. Grant, the common man in common garb, seemed truly to be the antithesis of Lee, the Southern aristocrat, and his popularity and fame at this juncture even overshadowed Lincoln's. His unremarkable face was known to every citizen in both North and South, and among blacks he was spoken of with reverence and even awe; Lincoln had freed the slaves, but Grant was liberating them. There was even talk of him running for president in the upcoming elections.

Rumors were circulating that Lincoln was going to ask Congress to pass an act reviving the rank of lieutenant general, last held by George Washington himself. Reportedly, the president intended to promote Grant to this, the ultimate military position. Grant, in the meantime, had established a headquarters in Nashville, Tennessee, and had brought his family west to join him. On March 4, 1864, he received a telegram from Lincoln ordering him to report to Washington immediately. Grant proceeded east with little fanfare. He took his 14-year-old son, Fred, along. On March 8, Grant and Lincoln, the two guardians of the Union, met face-to-face for the first time. The next morning the former clerk from Galena was made lieutenant general, commander of all the armies of the United States. There were now 850,000 troops under Grant's command, and only 1 man left in the country to whom Grant answered.

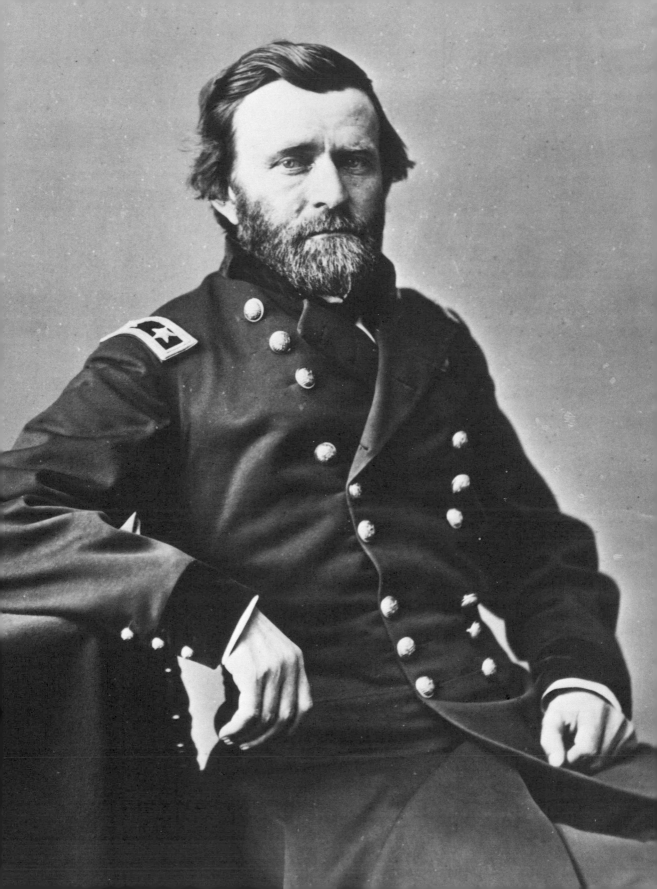

6

"The Murderous Work Went On"

In March 1864, Ulysses S. Grant and his family moved to Washington, D.C., and Grant assumed his duties as lieutenant general. From now on, Grant was to work closely with the president. Both men felt that the Confederate war effort was on the verge of collapsing and that a final, massive federal onslaught might prove to be the coup de grace. And indeed, in the past two years of the war the South had suffered several crucial setbacks. The fall of Vicksburg and the defeats at Gettysburg and Chattanooga had been telling blows, and the federal naval blockade of Southern ports (the Anaconda Plan) was slowly choking off the Confederacy and preventing it from receiving desperately needed supplies. Perhaps even more damaging to Southern morale was the Emancipation Proclamation, which as of January 1, 1863, made all slaves "thenceforward and forever free." The Emancipation Proclamation not only robbed the South of one of its key resources — slaves — but it effectively eliminated any

> *Whatever happens, there will be no turning back.*
> —ULYSSES S. GRANT
> to President Lincoln at the start of the Wilderness campaign

In the spring of 1864, Grant, now in command of all the federal armies, devised his grim plan to crush the Confederacy and bring the war to an end. His strategy was simple — to fight the enemy on all fronts, destroy their resources, and kill as many of them as possible.

General Sherman (at right, leaning on cannon) was a key component in Grant's plan to break the Southern rebellion once and for all. Sherman, at the head of an army of 80,000, was to march on Atlanta, Georgia, with orders to take — and destroy — the city.

chance of the Confederacy receiving recognition and aid from one of the European powers. Once Lincoln formally made the war between the states a crusade to end slavery, no other nation would risk supporting the side that was fighting in favor of the barbaric institution. The Emancipation Proclamation was the decisive political and psychological blow of the war.

The natural advantages that the North held over the South were also beginning to make a difference. The North had greater industrial resources and, perhaps most important of all, the North had more fighting men — many more. It was this basic advantage that Grant and Lincoln hoped to utilize as they plotted in the White House throughout March and April. A huge, coordinated offensive would be unleashed; the North would hammer the South on all fronts at once. Sherman, now at the head of the Army of the Cumberland, would storm into Georgia with 110,000 men and march on Atlanta. (Sherman relished his assignment, declaring "I can make Georgia howl!" as he set off.) In the meantime, General Nathaniel Prentiss Banks would advance on Mobile, Alabama, and into the Deep South, where he was to rendezvous with Sherman. General Franz Sigel would attempt to take control of the Shenandoah Valley, and General Benjamin Butler and his Army of the James would advance on Richmond, the Confederate capital, from the south. Grant left the hardest task for himself. With the massive Army of the Potomac — 120,000 troops — he would move into Virginia, find, and engage Robert E. Lee's seemingly indestructible Army of Northern Virginia. Grant and Lincoln knew that as long as Lee's army survived, so did the Confederacy. To break Lee's army was to break the back of the rebellion.

In the spring of 1864, Grant initiated one of the most brutal campaigns in military history. His strategy was simple and ruthlessly logical: He outnumbered his opponent two to one; therefore he would find his enemy, make him fight, and, through sheer weight of numbers, crush him. Thus began the Wilderness campaign, the final showdown between the two premier generals of the war. During this five-week series of almost apocalyptic battles, Lee was unyielding, and Grant was relentless. Between them, more than 50,000 men would die. "It was," Secretary of War Edwin M. Stanton said, "the bloodiest swath ever cut through this globe."

Grant (at left, leaning over the back of an adjutant to study a map) holds a council of war in Bethesda, Maryland, at the outset of the Wilderness campaign. His staff members are sitting on pews dragged from a local church.

Casualties of the Wilderness campaign in Virginia. The attrition rate for this campaign was staggering — in the first month there were more than 60,000 Union men killed or wounded — but Grant was relentless and continued to pressure Lee's army.

On May 3, Grant's huge force began crossing the Rapidan River into a desolate, heavily wooded area of Virginia known only as the Wilderness. Lee, reluctant to face Grant on open ground, had moved his army into the Wilderness in the hope that Grant would follow. Grant obliged, and the two armies stumbled upon one another on May 5. The battle that followed was a confused, nightmarish affair, as various regiments alternately confronted and pursued one another through the tangled brush. The woods were soon clogged with the smoke of battle, adding to the general confusion and terror. Soldiers crept through the fog, firing on anything that moved. Opposing regiments suddenly found themselves face to face; point-blank volleys were exchanged and aimless charges were mounted. In this manner the armies fought for two days. "It was a blind and bloody fight to the death," a Union private wrote. "The dead and wounded lay thick in the jungle of scrub-oaks, pines, and underbrush." At night, groups of lost men tried to find their way back to their regiments. Flash fires swept through the brush, and the forest was filled with the screams of the wounded as they were overtaken by the flames.

Grant's army suffered 17,000 casualties in the Battle of the Wilderness; Lee's army suffered half that many. Another Union general would have withdrawn at this point, and Lee felt that Grant would do just that. But Lee did not know Grant yet. Instead of retreating back over the Rapidan, Grant moved forward, toward Richmond, knowing that Lee would be forced to place his army between the federals and the Confederate capital. The men of the Army of the Potomac did not know Grant yet either. Under their previous commanders they had grown accustomed to being mauled by Lee and then retreating, and when they realized that Grant was moving them forward, not back, they set up a huge cheer that echoed throughout the woods. Lee, in the meantime, had decided to make a stand at the crossroads town of Spotsylvania Court House; Grant arrived there on May 9 to find his enemy firmly entrenched and waiting. On May 10, the federals attacked.

By all accounts, the Battle of Spotsylvania was the most horrid and bitterly contested event of the war. The trenches were soon filled with the dead men of both armies. A salient, or outward projection of the Confederate line, shaped like an arrowhead pointing toward the advancing Union troops, developed at the spot where Grant concentrated his attacks. Known as the Bloody Angle, this was a place of dreadful carnage, a crucible where thousands of men fought at close quarters amid ever growing piles of dead and wounded. "I know," a Confederate soldier who survived the Bloody Angle wrote after the war, "that along the sides and base of that angle the musketry fire is said to have been heavier than it ever was at any other place in all the world." Horace Porter, one of Grant's aides, provided his own description of the fighting around the Bloody Angle:

Grant (left, with papers in his right hand) and his staff at Cold Harbor, Virginia. Lee's troops inflicted a fearful beating on the Army of the Potomac at Cold Harbor in early June 1864.

"The battle near the angle was probably the most desperate engagement in the history of modern warfare, and presented features which were absolutely appalling. It was chiefly a savage hand-to-hand fight across the breastworks. Rank after rank was riddled by shot and shell and bayonet thrusts, and finally sank, a mass of torn and mutilated corpses; then fresh troops rushed madly forward to replace the dead, and so the murderous work went on." For nine days, sometimes from dawn to midnight, Grant hurled his men at the enemy entrenchments. A lethal hatred between the two armies manifested itself at Spotsylvania; the battle seemed to take on a terrible life of its own, and neither army wanted to yield or withdraw.

Finally, on the night of May 19, Grant quit Spotsylvania and moved his army around Lee's right flank; Lee moved with him and for the next 10 days the armies engaged in a cumbersome *danse macabre* across the Virginia landscape, stopping only to smash at one another along the North Anna River, at places with names like Hanover Junction and Sexton's Station, Dabney's Ferry and Pole Cat Creek. By June 1, the Army of Northern Virginia was once again squarely in between the Army of the Potomac and Richmond, at a place called Cold Harbor. At dawn on June 3, to the disbelief of General Lee, Grant unleashed yet another all-out assault on the rebel lines, hoping to smash through for a headlong rush on Richmond. Lee's troops, well protected behind strong fortifications, met the federal charge with murderous artillery and musket volleys. Within an hour, 7,000 Union troops lay killed or wounded — more than the total of Americans killed or wounded in the entire War of 1812. The Confederates suffered only 2,000 casualties. Grant called off the attack. The two armies, within shouting distance of one another, began to dig in again.

There was but one more move for Grant to make. In mid-June, under cover of darkness, he sidestepped to the left and began to cross the James River, using boats and a gigantic pontoon bridge. Lee was forced to fall back to protect his flank and the small town of Petersburg — the back door to

Richmond. There, the armies of Grant and Lee pounded each other for three more days. On June 18, both armies began to dig trenches, and a siege began.

The Wilderness campaign was over. Grant had not destroyed the Army of Northern Virginia, nor had he taken the Confederate capital. But he had checkmated his Southern rival. Lee was outnumbered, outmaneuvered, and the savage warfare of the past weeks had crippled his army. Any move he made at this point could only bring defeat. Although Lee had inflicted many more casualties — about 60,000 — on the Union army than they had inflicted on his troops, the federals quickly replaced their losses with reinforcements. (Many of the reinforcements were newly recruited black troops; more than 170,000 blacks would see action before the end of the war.) Lee, however, received no substantial reinforcements. At Petersburg, subsequently, he faced an Army of the Potomac that was almost as large as it had been at the beginning of the Wilderness campaign. The Army of Northern Virginia, on the other hand, had lost more than a third of its effectives — about 30,000 — and could not replace most of them. The Army of Northern Virginia had no hope of defeating Grant's army now, and to withdraw meant leaving Richmond undefended. Lee was pinned, and his army was out of the war.

Union troops entrenched outside the town of Petersburg, Virginia, in the spring of 1865. For Robert E. Lee's Army of Northern Virginia, Petersburg was the end of the road.

Many in the North were unhappy with the Wilderness campaign and its results. There had not been the decisive victory they hoped for; instead, the newspapers carried tales of inconclusive battles and appalling casualty rates. Grant was called a "butcher." Indeed, if one judged by the numbers of dead and wounded, Grant had been whipped from one end of Virginia to another. The Union campaigns on the other fronts had been less than conclusive as well. Sigel, Banks, and Butler had been unsuccessful, and Sherman's drive on Atlanta had bogged down in the face of fierce resistance by the army of General Joseph E. Johnston. Lincoln himself was nervous. Elections were approaching, and the antiwar Democrats, fueled by the public's disaffection with the war, were threatening to make a strong showing. It was conceivable that Lincoln could lose the election. If that happened, the new administration would most assuredly strike a treaty with the Confederacy — a treaty that would exclude any reunification of the Northern and Southern states.

But if everyone else in the North was on the verge of panic, Grant was not. He realized that now it was only a matter of time for the Confederacy as far as military matters were concerned. He was composed and quietly grim, almost to the point of cynicism, during this final period of the war. Shrugging off a brush with death — on August 10 he narrowly missed being blown to bits by a bomb smuggled into his tent by a rebel saboteur — Grant set up headquarters in a small cabin in City Point, Virginia, a little town near Petersburg, and began issuing the orders that would bring the war to its conclusion.

They were harsh directives, designed to break the will of an enemy that simply refused to give up. More men were needed; Lincoln put out a call for 500,000 fresh volunteers. To further exploit the disparity in numbers between North and South, Grant ordered an end to the practice of exchanging prisoners; he could replace any Union soldiers captured by the enemy — Lee could not. Sherman was to continue to pressure Atlanta; his presence there prevented any of the Confederate armies in the south from coming east in an attempt to relieve the bottled-up

Army of Northern Virginia. Rebel guerrilla activity in the Shenandoah Valley had to be crushed, particularly the mounted forces under General John S. Mosby and General Jubal Early. Grant sent Sheridan to do this job, with orders to imprison all non-enlisted male citizens known to be hostile to the Union, along with the family members of known guerrillas. Any rebel raiders caught out of uniform were to be executed summarily. He also gave Sheridan instructions to destroy anything that could be construed as being an aid to the Confederate war effort — crops, farmland, railroad tracks, telegraph lines, working plantations, administrative buildings, and headquarters. Livestock and all food stores were to be confiscated, and any slaves still held were to be liberated. "We want the Shenandoah Valley to remain a barren waste," Grant told Sheridan. The cavalry commander went about this job with great efficiency. Grant's policy of total war had begun.

But Grant was also looking back over his shoulder, at Washington, D.C. He knew as well as anyone else that if Lincoln lost the election, all their efforts to preserve the Union would come to naught. One big, decisive, unequivocal victory before the November elections might convince the voters that the end was in sight; that Lincoln, if reelected, would indeed defeat the Confederacy and preserve the Union. It was Sherman who provided this most necessary triumph. On September 2, 1864, Grant received a telegram from Sherman: "Atlanta is ours, and fairly won." Lincoln declared a national day of thanksgiving. Two months later he was elected to a second term of office.

Now the victories came one after another as the Confederacy began to crumble on all fronts. Sheridan, the scourge of the Shenandoah, wiped the valley clean of all Confederate resistance. The Army of Tennessee — the last major Confederate force aside from the Army of Northern Virginia — was broken at the Battle of Nashville by the Union forces of Generals Thomas and Schofield. And Sherman, leaving Atlanta in flames behind him, was engaged in his infamous march to the sea. As his massive army moved through the heartland of the South they im-

In August 1864, Grant put General Philip H. Sheridan in command of the Army of the Shenandoah and sent him into the Shenandoah Valley with instructions to pursue the enemy "to the death."

plemented the same tactics that Sheridan had used in the Shenandoah, but on a much grander scale. Attila-like, Sherman destroyed everything in his path and left great conflagrations in his wake. When a group of Southern politicians made a gentlemanly appeal to Sherman to stop his destructive tactics, the general replied that "war is cruelty and you cannot refine it. You might as well appeal against the thunder-storm as against these terrible hardships of war." And Sherman was war personified during these final days of the Southern rebellion. Implacable, commanding his rough troops with a cynical good humor (they called him Uncle Billy), he reached Savannah in December, and as the new year began, he turned and started out for South Carolina. Sherman intended to punish that state — it had been the first to secede from the Union.

For Grant, there was nothing left to do but wait for Lee's final, obligatory attempt to break free from Petersburg and escape to the west or south. Grant had never tolerated waiting very well, and as spring approached and Sherman's juggernaut moved inexorably north, toward Richmond, the lieutenant general was plagued by migraines and sleeplessness.

The ruins of the Confederate capital of Richmond, Virginia, as seen from across the James River. As the victorious Union troops entered the city on April 3, 1865, freed slaves danced for joy in the streets.

Finally, in early April, as all of Grant's armies converged on Virginia, Lee executed the final, token troop movements; they were easily and swiftly halted by Sheridan's men. On the morning of April 9, after yet another sleepless night, Grant received a message from Lee requesting terms of surrender. Later that afternoon, Secretary of War Stanton, in the capital, received a devastatingly simple telegram from Grant: "General Lee surrendered the Army of Northern Virginia this afternoon on terms proposed by myself." Following the surrender, Grant collected his family and went to Washington to participate in a conference with Lincoln and his cabinet. On Friday, April 14, after a long discussion in the White House, Lincoln invited Grant and Julia to accompany him and the first lady to a play at Ford's Theater that evening. Grant declined; he knew that Julia disliked Mrs. Lincoln, and he wanted to spend the evening alone with his wife anyway.

Sherman, Grant, Lincoln, and Porter (left to right) meet on March 28, 1865, on board the *River Queen*, anchored off City Point, Virginia. Lincoln was assassinated on April 14.

7

"I Shall Have No Policy"

The Civil War was over, and Ulysses S. Grant, still a relatively young man at 43, was once again a lost soul. War had saved Grant from the pit of poverty and obscurity he had fallen into; now the war was gone and once more Grant stood, befuddled, on the edge of that terribly familiar abyss. He had absolutely no idea about what to do with himself once the war was done; all he knew was that he must keep as much distance as possible between himself and the social and financial void of the prewar days. But if Grant had no idea what to do with himself after the war, everybody else in America did: They were all talking about Grant becoming president. Julia was talking about Grant becoming president; Babcock and Rawlins and Jesse Root Grant were talking about Grant becoming president; Sherman was talking about Grant becoming president; and

> *There is no country where the energetic man can, by his own labor, and by his own industry, ingenuity, and frugality, acquire competency as he can in America.*
> —ULYSSES S. GRANT

Following the conclusion of the Civil War and the assassination of Lincoln, Grant became the most famous and popular man in the United States. Americans looked to him as a symbol of national unity, and in 1868 he was elected president.

President Andrew Johnson was already trying to figure out how to prevent Grant from becoming president. Lincoln was gone, and Grant was seen as the savior of the republic; he became the symbol of national unity and strength that Americans focused on. Much of the adulation that would, and should, have gone to Lincoln, the true genius of the age, instead fell on Grant's shoulders. Even in the South he was regarded with respect, partially because of his graceful behavior toward Lee and his army at Appomattox, and partially because Southerners were directing most of their hatred toward the great bogey Sherman, and toward the freedmen. Grant listened to the talk and soon determined that he *must* become president, even though he knew in his heart that he had no business entering politics. Ulysses S. Grant was a professional soldier, a great leader of other professional soldiers — he was no politician, no leader of a nation, no Lincoln. But he had risen to such heights, such fame and popularity, that it seemed to him that a step in any direction other than toward the White House would be a step backward, a step downward, and he could not let the inexorable slide begin again. So, as talk of the presidency swirled around him and the Democrats and Republicans courted his favor, Grant, with a kind of simpleminded cunning, kept his mouth shut and let the tide carry him along toward the Oval Office.

And his fame and popularity were so great during the years immediately following the war that even his own political naïveté was not enough to mess things up completely, although he managed to come close. In 1867 he allowed himself to be used as a pawn in the feud between the Radical Republican–dominated Congress and President Johnson — a feud that ultimately led to impeachment proceedings against Johnson. The president was trying to dismiss Secretary of War Stanton; Congress needed Stanton just where he was because he was the only member of the executive branch who was favorably disposed toward the Radical Republicans' progressive Reconstruction programs. Congress asserted that under the tenets of the Tenure of Office Act,

Andrew Johnson became president following the assassination of Lincoln in 1865. In 1867, Grant became involved in the feud between Johnson and Congress that eventually led to impeachment proceedings against Johnson.

the president could not dismiss a member of his cabinet without congressional approval. They did not approve of a dismissal of Stanton; Johnson fired him anyway and then offered the post of secretary of war *ad interim* to Grant. The president believed that Congress would be unwilling to attempt a removal of Grant because of the general's great prestige, and that Grant could hold down the office until the Supreme Court got around to voting on the Tenure of Office Act — Johnson was sure the act would be ruled unconstitutional. Grant went along with Johnson's scheme. But when push came to shove,

First Lady Julia Grant in the White House. Even after Grant had lost his bid for a third term, Mrs. Grant felt that the presidential mansion was her true home.

Grant, fearful of making an enemy of Congress and damaging his own presidential prospects, abandoned Johnson. For this he received a brutal face-to-face lambasting from the president and some unfavorable press. However, he emerged from the fiasco relatively unscathed and was nominated as the Republican presidential candidate.

Grant fully expected to be elected president — there was never any question about his popularity with the public — and he carried the vote, defeating Democrat Horatio Seymour. The house-proud Julia finally had the kind of home she had always felt she and her husband deserved. (As they moved into the White House in March 1869, Grant, with his wry sense of humor, turned to his wife and said, "My dear, I hope you're satisfied now.") Grant purchased a dapper new wardrobe in New York, smoked a lot of cigars, projected an air of quiet competence, and wondered what to do now that he was president of the United States.

In truth, Grant did not know what to do. Back in May 1868, when he was nominated, Grant began his acceptance speech by saying, "I shall have no policy of my own to interfere against the will of the people." Although he qualified the first part of this statement, it is that part that gives an accurate indication of Grant's approach to the presidency: He had no policy. He had no real vision of the future of his country; he had not aspired to the office to implement any substantial changes that he believed in deeply; rather, he saw it as a good job opportunity, an administrative position that would provide him with a house, a good salary, and a chance to meet influential and wealthy people who might help him when this job was over. The guiding force during his presidency would be an aversion to any form of social disorder; now that he had attained a higher socioeconomic status, he feared any large mass of discontented people, be they black or white. Rather than make an attempt to help those people — he of all presidents should have identified with their plight — he warded them off entirely, as if any contact with them would contaminate him or suck him back down into their penniless and begrimed midst. Behind everything he did following the war, there lurked the haunting specter of a man in shabby clothes reduced to selling firewood on a cold St. Louis street corner. What few ideas he did come up with during his eight years as president were vague, occasionally good hearted, and sometimes bizarre. Those that did have merit were destined to be undermined by corruption, bureaucratic incompetence, or sheer political inertia.

A more experienced cabinet would have helped. The names that a baffled Senate was confronted with as the new president filled his key posts inspired quizzical expressions on faces all around the country. Grant chose friends, officers from the war,

Grant receives a delegation of American Indians in May 1870. In his inaugural address, Grant promised fair treatment for the "original occupants of this land," but in reality, the Native Americans received only lip service from Grant.

wealthy men he admired, and small-time politicos to help him run the country. A few of his appointments were good ones. Hamilton Fish, the man Grant appointed as secretary of state, was a refined East Coast blue blood who was to serve the administration skillfully for both terms. John A. Rawlins of Galena, Grant's best friend and guardian angel, was made secretary of war. Rawlins, who had served Grant faithfully throughout the war, was brilliant, dynamic, incorruptible, and compassionate, and he could have made a huge difference during the next eight years, especially in the areas of Reconstruction and Indian policy. Unfortunately, he died of tuberculosis in September 1869, and Grant never found his equal as a friend or adviser.

If there was an issue that seemed to be close to Grant's heart, it was the plight of the people he referred to as the "original occupants of this land," the Native Americans. Before the war, when he was stationed in the Northwest, Grant had seen the deplorable conditions under which many of the Indians lived. As president, Grant felt that he was in a position to help them, and he made an attempt to do so. His sentiments were noble, but his actions were ill conceived and somewhat weak; he never threw the whole weight of his reputation and office behind them. He made a good start by appointing an Indian — Ely S. Parker, a Seneca who had been on Grant's staff during the war — as commissioner of Indian affairs, but Parker's effectiveness was limited by white politicians who felt that they were more fit than a "mere Indian" to handle the welfare of the Indians. The programs that Grant initiated to help the Indians — the Peace Policy and the Quaker Policy — were unimaginative and lacking in a true understanding of the Indians. The programs simply confined them to reservations and placed the administration of the reservations in the hands of priests and missionaries, whose job it would be to "civilize" the Indians (while converting them to Christianity in the meantime). More important than these halfhearted attempts to assimilate the Indians was the president's complete failure to stop the genocide being perpetrated on the tribes by the U.S. Army. Supposedly, it was the army's duty to protect settlers from the "savages"; in reality, men such as Sherman and Sheridan (who were still practicing total war and had simply found new enemies) and George Armstrong Custer (who would pay dearly for his transgressions) were systematically wiping them out. A strong stance on Grant's part certainly would have curtailed the atrocities, but such a stance was not forthcoming. The blankets and Bibles supplied by his Quaker and Peace policies could not stop the bullets fired by his armies.

Grant's presidency is remembered best for its political scandals and corruption; newspaper circulation thrived during those years as scandals

Major General George Armstrong Custer. While Grant was making promises to the Indians in Washington, men such as Custer were killing them off in the West.

bloomed like wild mushrooms on the White House lawn. Grant was not corrupt, but he was continually taken advantage of by those who were. The first scandal broke not long after Grant took office. A 61-year-old financier named Abel Rathbone Corbin had married Grant's 37-year-old sister, Jennie. Two unscrupulous associates of Corbin's, Wall Street financiers Jay Gould and James Fisk, Jr., used this connection to get close to Julia and Ulysses Grant. Grant and his secretary of the Treasury, George S. Boutwell, were about to initiate a program of financial retrenchment by removing greenbacks (paper money) from circulation, selling a large amount of federal gold, and replacing the greenbacks with a strictly gold-backed currency. Fisk and Gould, who were making a killing speculating on the gold market, needed things to stay the way they were; they got to Grant and talked him out of Boutwell's retrenchment plan. These fellows even got Julia Grant, Babcock, and other members of Grant's administration involved in the speculation, hoping Grant would avoid Boutwell's policy because it might harm the rather substantial investments of

President Grant (seated at the head of the table) meets with his cabinet in 1869. From left to right are Jacob D. Cox, Hamilton Fish, John A. Rawlins, John A. J. Creswell, George S. Boutwell, Adolph E. Borie, and Ebenezer R. Hoar.

his friends and his wife. When Grant finally figured out what was going on, he immediately implemented Boutwell's plan. Gould's subsequent, panicky withdrawal from the market resulted in an overall panic on the gold market known as Black Friday. Banks collapsed, speculators went broke, congressional hearings were called for. The Grants themselves were not implicated, but the president failed to learn a lesson from the incident, and Black Friday was only the first in a gaudy, eight-year parade of scandals.

Ironically, the ugliest blot on Ulysses Grant's presidential record was his failure to protect the very people he had done so much for in the Civil War — the black citizens of the United States. During the war, Grant had been the man to assume the responsibility of sending hundreds of thousands of Americans to their death in order to protect and ensure the promise of freedom that Lincoln had held out to the slaves. But when the time came for him to follow through on this promise and protect and enforce the Constitution once again; when the time came for him to see that the sacrifice of all those brave young men and of Lincoln himself was not an empty one; when the time came for him to make sure that all the death and destruction was not meaningless—he failed.

Grant seemed to want to do these things, to be a strong executive and back up unequivocally the civil rights legislation—the Thirteenth, Fourteenth, and Fifteenth Amendments, the Civil Rights Act of 1866, the enforcement bill of 1870 — that the Radical Republicans in Congress had passed since the war, but he simply would not take the risk. While blacks in the South were being lynched and maimed, terrorized and murdered, and while the old racist system of the South reentrenched itself like Lee's army at Petersburg, Grant responded with the kind of bland inaction that mocked his own boldness and courage during the war.

There is no doubt that he was the man who commanded the respect, authority, and power to flex strong federal muscles and crush the activity of the Ku Klux Klan, now so widespread, arrogant, and

His imperturbability is amazing. I am in doubt whether to call it greatness or stupidity.
—JAMES A. GARFIELD
on Grant as president

officially tolerated in the South that it constituted a second rebellion. And yet he did not. He made some token gestures and showed the occasional spark of his old self — in October 1871 he suspended habeas corpus in nine Klan-infested South Carolina counties and sent in federal troops to protect the black citizens, and in 1874 he sent troops under Sheridan into Louisiana for the same reason — but for the most part, instead of confronting the problem, he tried to get around it altogether. It was toward this end that he initiated his strange attempt to annex the island of Santo Domingo. Once he had possession of the island, the president planned to make it a refuge for all the discontented blacks in America. Grant was oddly obsessed with this idea, and he pursued it with more vigor than anything else during his presidency, but Congress blocked his efforts continually.

The motivation behind Grant's behavior during his first term of office was simple — he was afraid to do anything controversial, anything that would make people angry, anything that might cost him a second term. He was afraid to lose his job, and for once, at least, he did not. He was reelected in 1872, defeating the nominee of the Liberal Republican coalition, publisher Horace Greeley. Grant's second term of office was no different from his first — if anything, things got worse. The slaughter of the Native Americans continued in the West, the white-supremacist Democrats tightened their stranglehold on the South, corruption within the administration continued to besmirch Grant's reputation, and the economy collapsed, precipitating a depression that outlasted Grant's term. Grant consistently took the politically safe approach in dealing with these problems — he expected to be elected to a third term, although Republican leaders were quickly coming to the conclusion that Grant would have to be jettisoned for the good of the party. In failing to make a strong stand on the social and economic illnesses that were wracking the nation, Grant failed the very people who had elected him — newly enfranchised blacks and the members of the working class, including the thousands of Civil War veterans who had fallen on hard times in the depression.

By the summer of 1876 there was no one around the White House who gave a damn about the black people.
—WILLIAM S. McFEELY
historian, on the
Grant administration

Grant had campaigned under "The Workingman's Banner," and the workingman, black and white, had elected him. Grant rewarded his supporters by adopting conservative economic and Reconstruction policies that put the burden of the depression on the shoulders of working-class whites and that left southern blacks at the mercy of their white oppressors.

The final years of Grant's presidency were dominated by the notorious Whiskey Ring scandal. The scandal involved Treasury officials being bribed by liquor distributors in return for illegal tax breaks given on large volumes of liquor. A congressional investigation of the liquor frauds led right into Grant's backyard, where his trusted aide and closest remaining friend, Orville Babcock, was exposed. Publicly, the president never acknowledged the guilt of his old friend, which seemed to be obvious to everyone in the country except Grant himself; he even testified before the chief justice in Babcock's behalf. Privately, the knowledge of this betrayal cut Grant to the quick; when he received indisputable evidence implicating Babcock, the president wept bitterly.

In an 1871 cartoon, "Marm" Grant pleads with Uncle Sam for another four years in the White House; Sam would rather have presidential candidate Horace Greeley living there. Grant was reelected.

8

America's Guests

Ulysses and Julia Grant were homeless once again. Having failed to gain the Republican nomination for the 1876 election — it went to Rutherford B. Hayes — the Grants moved out of the White House and became the nation's, and eventually the world's, most well-known and high-living vagabonds. They traveled about the country, going from one honorary banquet to the next, living in hotels and guest rooms and guest houses. As president, Grant had been repudiated and his political credit was exhausted; as "the General," he was still the most famous man in America, and his popular credit seemed unlimited. The upper crust of American society adopted the strangely childlike couple. Homeless and jobless, their children grown and occupied with their own life, the Grants lived as America's guests and grew comfortably stout from one testimonial dinner after another.

> *Man proposes, God disposes.*
> —ULYSSES S. GRANT

Ulysses S. Grant, dying of throat cancer, works on his memoirs on the front porch of the house on Mount McGregor, New York, where the general spent his final days.

The Grants (front row, third and fourth from the left) visit a pyramid in Egypt in 1878. Following Grant's unsuccessful bid for a third term, the former president and his wife embarked on a world tour.

In May 1877 the Grants embarked upon what would become a two-year world tour. They wandered from country to country, continent to continent in an aimless and almost desperate fashion, haunted by their own lack of direction and the absence of a place they could call their own. But the most remarkable aspect of their tour was the reception they received in certain places, which provided Grant with some of the most gratifying moments of his life. To the amazement, and growing satisfaction, of Grant and his wife, massive crowds turned out to see him, especially in the working-class districts of the industrial cities of Great Britain. To these people, who had closely followed the news of the great and terrible conflict across the Atlantic, the American Civil War had been a class struggle, a war of liberation, and Grant had been the war's great liberator, the man who had emerged from the ranks of the proletariat to lead the huge republican armies in blue, a Napoleon who had never abused the awesome power he wielded; Grant had simply laid it down when his task was done. And so they thronged in the streets to see and hear the man who had freed the slaves. They came, hundreds of thousands of them, in places such as Birmingham and Glasgow, Newcastle and Edinburgh, the oppressed and the impoverished and the downtrodden, the miners and the factory workers and the dock laborers. And, perhaps, the outpouring of admiration they bestowed upon Grant helped him to remember, if only for a moment, who he really was.

The Grants came home in December 1879. They were fatter, older (almost 60), and, most importantly, poorer. Grant needed his old job back; Julia wanted "her" house back. It seemed obvious to them that Grant should be president once again; the people of Europe certainly would have elected him — why not the people of America? Grant felt that his two-year absence had given the voters enough time to forget about his scandal-ridden eight years in the White House and to arrive at the conclusion that Grant was the man for the job. Unfortunately, his party did not share his opinion and he lost the Republican nomination to James Garfield in 1880.

General Li Hung-chang of China and General Grant sit for a photograph in Tientsin, China, in 1878. "You and I, General Grant," Li said to his guest, "are the greatest men in the world." Like Grant, Li had suppressed a bloody rebellion in his country.

Ulysses ("Buck") Grant, Jr., invited his father to join the Wall Street brokerage firm of Grant & Ward in 1883. When the firm collapsed under a cloud of suspicion, Grant was once again penniless.

The decline of the general had begun. From this point on, his situation, both economic and physical, would deteriorate steadily. He began looking for a job suitable to a man of his stature. But Grant's judgment (and luck) in the world of business had not changed. In 1881 he accepted what looked like a lucrative and promising position as president of the new Mexican Southern Railroad, and he and Julia settled into an excellent house on Fifth Avenue in Manhattan. The builder of the railroad, Matías Romero of Mexico, felt that Grant's monolithic reputation and political connections would make him the perfect public-relations man and ensure the railroad's success and expansion into the Southwest. But by 1883 the Mexican Southern had gone bankrupt (through no fault of Grant's), and the former president was once again pounding the pavement.

Grant now found what seemed to be the position that would end his lifelong search for employment and allow him and his wife to live out the rest of their life in a suitable manner. Instead, the job brought Grant his final and ultimate humiliation and returned him to a state very much like the one he had been in just before the outbreak of the war. Back then, the war had saved him; this time, the same war would save him once again, but in a different way.

In 1881, Ulysses ("Buck") Grant, Jr., and Ferdinand Ward, the brilliant son of an upstate New York preacher, had formed the Wall Street brokerage firm of Grant & Ward. The new firm was immediately successful and Grant & Ward was soon being recognized as the next big brokerage house. When the general, at the invitation of his up-and-coming son, invested his life savings in the firm and became a full partner, Wall Street pundits agreed that his name would only add to the firm's growing reputation and success. For Grant and Julia, the new position seemed a godsend, and Grant felt a particular satisfaction — he was now a wealthy man of business, a member of the elite East Coast fraternity of Wall Street. But Buck Grant apparently had no more luck, or wisdom, in choosing business partners than his father had. Ward and the silent partner in the firm, James Fish, a bank president, had achieved their rapid and spectacular success through deft — and illegal — misrepresentations of their own credit status. In May 1884, Buck, the general, and a number of horrified investors learned that the supposed financial strength of the firm, much like Grant's dreams of financial security, was only a chimera created by Fish and Ward. Grant & Ward, Fish's bank, and a number of other brokerage houses folded faster than the Union troops at Bull Run, and with them went Ulysses Grant's life savings and another large chunk of his reputation.

Grant had come full circle. He was broke and unemployed, and his good name had taken a beating. Now he needed another call to arms, another Fort Sumter, another Vicksburg. He needed to return to the only place in which he had ever excelled — the battlefield. And, like the Grant who was surrounded at Belmont, the Grant who was besieged at Chattanooga, he found a way. He would write a book.

General Grant conducted his final campaign with pen and paper. In the summer of 1883, he had written two articles for *Century Magazine* on Shiloh and Vicksburg. The editors at *Century* were impressed with Grant's writing. It was lucid, direct, understated, and it broke down the seemingly chaotic elements of battle into a logical and understandable order. With none other than Samuel Clemens — Mark Twain — acting as his agent and literary mentor (Clemens had recognized immediately the merits of Grant's two *Century* articles), Grant signed a large contract with a publisher. With his financial situation finally resolved, he sat down to write his memoirs.

He spent his final year at a desk in the house in Manhattan and then at another desk in a small house in the Adirondack Mountains in upstate New York, writing steadily. The book, more than 500 pages long, has the same uninterrupted focus, the same concentration and clarity of vision that the general used in winning the great conflict. All outside concerns are gone, there is no talk of his days as a president or a clerk or a world traveler; all this is cast off, burned away by the terrible urgency, the

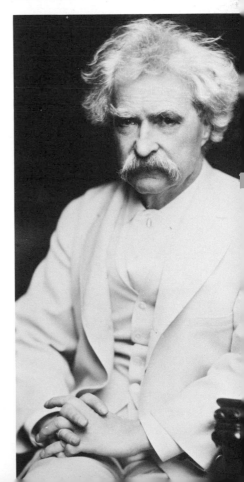

American writer and humorist Samuel Clemens was largely responsible for the publication of the *Personal Memoirs of U.S. Grant.* Grant finished writing the book only nine days before his death.

Grant (center, sitting in chair) and his family gather on the front porch of the house on Mount McGregor. Each day hundreds of tourists would file past, hoping to get a glimpse of the general.

terrible immediacy, of war. The reader of Grant's memoirs experiences this immediacy and finds out what it would have been like to serve under Grant, and what it was that made him a great soldier and a greater general. And Grant, returning to the scenes of battle, to Fort Donelson and Vicksburg, to the Wilderness and Spotsylvania, was allowed to find himself once again.

As he wrote, Ulysses S. Grant slowly died, as if in writing about the experience that had given his life meaning and purpose he was also expelling it, so that when he finished there was nothing left inside him and he simply died. (It was not bullets or bayonets that killed the warrior but too many cigars; he died of throat cancer.) On July 23, 1885, Ulysses S. Grant, commander of all the armies of the United States, passed away. He had no last words. His book was published to great popular and critical acclaim. Samuel Clemens called it the finest military memoir since Caesar wrote about Gaul.

Ulysses S. Grant was something of an enigma when he lived, and he remains enigmatic, and almost inscrutable, in death. Perhaps William T. Sherman, one of the men who knew Grant best, summed up the elusive nature of the man when he wrote that "Grant's whole character was a mystery even to himself — a combination of strength and weakness not paralleled by any of whom I have read in Ancient or Modern history." And so far, Grant's place in American history has been unsure, although his rags-to-riches-to-rags story is uniquely American, as is the understated, matter-of-fact courage he brought to situations of the most frightening turmoil and terror. In the century since the Civil War, he has been obscured by Lincoln's ever-lengthening shadow, and the reputation he developed as a failure, a drunk, and a callous butcher of human lives has dogged him. He was a failure — in the world of capital and politics, at least — and he

In late March 1885, Grant seemed close to death. He rallied, however, and was able to resume his normal routine. His doctor was "inclined to attribute" the remission "to the brandy" Grant had been drinking.

did drink. But he was no more a butcher than Eisenhower, who sent thousands of Americans charging up the beach to their doom at Normandy, or MacArthur, who urged his troops into the tropical hornets' nests of Iwo Jima and Okinawa, or Pershing, who committed thousands of untried American troops to the nightmarish trench and gas warfare of the western front during World War I. In truth, Grant was the only Union general with the moral courage to fight the war in the manner required to win the war. Nobody, not even Lincoln, wanted to accept this responsibility. But Grant, and the men who fought under him, embraced it. He had an innate, and even intimate, understanding of the true nature of warfare; he made no pretenses about this and he made no apologies either, and for that he gained the reputation of a butcher. Grant himself remained perplexed to the end of his days by politicians — and the citizens who elect them — who clamor for war and then seek to place blame when people get killed.

Grant died on July 23, 1885. A massive funeral ceremony was held in New York, and Grant's body was escorted up Fifth Avenue by an honor guard of officers from both the Confederate and Union armies.

Grant's Tomb, overlooking the Hudson River as it flows past New York City, was completed in 1897 and is the final resting place of the general and his wife.

In the end, Grant is best understood as one of those strange figures who appear, either by providence or through some process of historical necessity, at a time when they, and only they, can accomplish a certain task. There was probably no other man alive in the United States who was equipped with the peculiar characteristics that allowed Ulysses S. Grant to win the Civil War. In making a final judgment on his value as a general and an American, this question must always be posed: What would the United States be like today if Grant and his armies had not defeated the Confederacy?

Further Reading

Anderson, Dwight Scott, and Nancy Scott Anderson. *The Generals—Ulysses S. Grant and Robert E. Lee.* New York: Random House, 1988.

Bruns, Roger. *Abraham Lincoln.* New York: Chelsea House, 1986.

Cadwallader, Sylvanus. *Three Years with Grant, as Recalled by War Correspondent Sylvanus Cadwallader.* New York: Knopf, 1955.

Catton, Bruce. *Grant Moves South.* Boston: Little, Brown, 1960.

———. *Grant Takes Command.* Boston: Little, Brown, 1960.

———. *U. S. Grant and the American Military Tradition.* Boston: Little, Brown, 1954.

Frassanito, William A. *Grant and Lee: The Virginia Campaigns, 1864–1865.* New York: Scribners, 1983.

Frost, Lawrence A. *U. S. Grant Album: A Pictorial Biography of Ulysses S. Grant.* Seattle: Bonanza Books, 1974.

Goldhurst, Richard. *Many Are the Hearts: The Agony and the Triumph of Ulysses S. Grant.* New York: Reader's Digest, 1975.

Grant, Julia Dent. *The Personal Memoirs of Julia Dent Grant.* Edited by John Y. Simon. New York: Putnam, 1975.

Grant, Ulysses S. *The Personal Memoirs of U. S. Grant.* New York: The Century Co., 1895.

Hoelig, A. A. *Vicksburg, 47 Days of Siege.* Englewood Cliffs, NJ: Prentice-Hall, 1969.

King, Perry Scott. *Jefferson Davis.* New York: Chelsea House, 1990.

Lewis, Lloyd. *Captain Sam Grant.* New York: Little, Brown, 1950.

McFeely, William S. *Grant: A Biography.* New York: Norton, 1981.

Miers, Earl Sebeneck. *The Last Campaign: Grant Saves the Union.* Philadelphia: Lippincott, 1972.

———. *The Web of Victory: Grant at Vicksburg.* New York: Knopf, 1955.

Smith, Gene. *Lee and Grant: A Dual Biography.* New York: McGraw-Hill, 1984.

Chronology

April 27, 1822	Born Hiram Ulysses Grant in Point Pleasant, Ohio
1839–43	Attends U.S. Military Academy at West Point
1845–48	Serves under General Zachary Taylor and General Winfield Scott in Mexican War
1848	Promoted to first lieutenant upon return to the United States and later marries Julia Dent
May 1850	Julia gives birth to the first of four children, Frederick Dent Grant
1854	Grant resigns from the army under charges of alcoholism
1860	Abraham Lincoln elected president
1861	Confederate forces attrack Fort Sumter; Civil War begins; Grant is appointed colonel in Illinois militia and later is promoted to brigadier general
1862	Gains national attention by capturing Fort Donelson; Battle of Shiloh takes place, the bloodiest fighting yet of the war
1863	Lincoln issues Emancipation Proclamation on New Year's Day; in July, Grant captures Vicksburg and is promoted to major general
1864	Meets Lincoln for the first time; promoted to lieutenant general of Union army; leads Army of the Potomac into Virginia; begins Wilderness campaign to defeat General Lee; Sherman marches through Georgia, taking Atlanta; Lincoln reelected
1865	Lee surrenders at Appomattox
1868	Grant elected 18th president of the United States
1872	Reelected president
1873	Nationwide depression begins
1874–76	Grant administration wracked with charges of corruption; Grant loses the Republican nomination to Rutherford B. Hayes
1877–79	Travels with Julia around the world
1880	Decides to run for president for a third time; Republicans nominate James A. Garfield instead
1881	Grant accepts position as president of Mexican Southern Railroad only to see it go bankrupt two years later
1884	Loses life savings in son's failed Wall Street brokerage firm
1884–85	Writes *The Personal Memoirs of U.S. Grant*
July 23, 1885	Dies of throat cancer at the age of 63

Index

Steven O'Brien has taught high school social studies in Massachusetts for nearly 20 years. He holds an M.A. in history from the University of Connecticut as well as a certificate of advanced study and a Ph.D. from Harvard. The author of *Alexander Hamilton* in the Chelsea House series WORLD LEADERS—PAST AND PRESENT, his writing has appeared in the *New York Times Magazine* and other publications.

Arthur M. Schlesinger, jr., taught history at Harvard for many years and is currently Albert Schweitzer Professor of the Humanities at City University of New York. He is the author of numerous highly praised works in American history and has twice been awarded the Pulitzer Prize. He served in the White House as special assistant to Presidents Kennedy and Johnson.
